THE AMERICAN CANON

DANIEL L. MARSH
President of Boston University

ABINGDON—COKESBURY PRESS
NEW YORK   NASHVILLE

MARSH
THE AMERICAN CANON

Copyright, 1939, by
DANIEL L. MARSH

CONTENTS

PREFACE

SOME sixteen or eighteen years ago, following the World War, I started the study that has resulted in this book. The reason for making the study was because the patriotism that had been generated for and by the War took all sorts of peculiar forms after the War was over.

The situation furnished abundant evidence that in the political realm, no less than in the physical, action and reaction are equal. Some sincere patriots became so zealous in their defense of what they thought was essential to the safeguarding of America that they manifested an un-American spirit. On the other hand, certain persons who were secret or open disciples of Communist and Fascist promulgators of subversive doctrines took advantage of the confusion for the dissemination of un-Americanism under the guise of liberal Americanism. Intolerance and bigotry stalked with both groups. Patriotic societies, old and new, proclaimed aloud their tenets, which were as likely to be errors born of ignorance as truths born of intelligence. It became the style to call names. Men and women grew hysterical, and proscribed and persecuted those with whom they did not agree, impugning their motives and tarring them with the stick of opprobrium. Professional patriots appeared, self-seeking persons who affected the livery of patriotism for the sake of political preferment. The very elect were often deceived.

I felt, as I am certain others did, the need of something that would give us the definitive distinctions of true American patriotism. Surely, somewhere there were some documents that all Americans would accept as the undisputed creed, or

5

"Bible," of Americanism. So, on my own account, I started to study the question. In odds and ends of time, I worked for a number of years in making a comparative study of great American pronouncements of one kind and another, sifting them out by a testing process, even as it seemed to me ancient scholars might have tested various writings when they were deciding which ones should finally be included in the New Testament, for instance.

I finally chose the seven writings that are included in this volume. Then I began research into their origin, antecedents, history, and implications. I pursued the study, in fragments of time, down to the present. Meantime, arrogancy and fear continued to thicken the confusion in which the public mind weltered, until today the distortions of patriotism are worse than they were immediately following the War. Therefore I decided to use the gist of my findings as my Baccalaureate Sermon to the Boston University Class of 1939. The multitude who heard the Baccalaureate Sermon, both those who thronged Symphony Hall and those who listened over the radio, showed an eager and earnest appreciation of the point of view expressed. The attention given to the message by the public press, both in the news columns and on the editorial pages, seemed to indicate that the study was timely. Thus I was encouraged to expand the Baccalaureate Sermon —or, rather, to condense the result of years of study—into the present volume.

We need something that will set the standard of American patriotism. Can it be done better than by these great documents that are accepted by all Americans? Let us have peace! Let us have intelligence! I hope my fellow Americans will read THE AMERICAN CANON, not because I have written it, but because I believe it is so vastly important that Americans, young and old, should honestly know what Americanism is, and because I faithfully believe that it is revealed in the documents submitted herewith. Then we shall walk in the light as the authors of these seven immortal documents were in the light. We shall have fellowship one with another as we walk the high road away from confusion and hysteria, and America will realize the dream of social progress which she cherishes in her heart.

DANIEL L. MARSH.

Boston University,
August 11, 1939.

THE AMERICAN CANON

BY THE AMERICAN CANON, I do not mean some new collection of the books of the Bible, like the *Palestinian Canon* or the *Alexandrian Canon*. I am using the term, rather, in an analogical sense, to say that there are certain American writings so significant, so inspired, so esteemed by Americans, so durably valuable to the American people, so pregnant with the essence of the American spirit, so revelatory of the genius of America, that, taken together, they constitute the authoritative rule of Americanism.

I have selected seven such writings. There is no eighth. I have been studying them for many years, and have long felt that if they were collected into a single volume, accompanied by simple exposition, they would constitute the best possible textbook for the making of intelligent citizens.

The Bible has a universal appeal and application, and its canon is sacred. These seven writings to which I refer have an American appeal and application, and, of course, are secular. However, let me sustain the analogy with the canonical books of the Bible while I name these American writings.

1. The genesis of American democracy is in the Mayflower Compact. In the beginning was the Pilgrim colony with that positive, original, social Compact which is the legitimate source of government.

2. Our exodus is in the Declaration of Independence. That immortal document marks the going out of the American people from tyrannical bondage to the promised land of liberty and self-government.

3. Our book of the law is the Constitution of the United

States. The counterpart of the Mosaic Ten Commandments in the political history of America is our Bill of Rights, the first ten amendments to the Constitution of the United States. The Ten Commandments of the Old Testament uttered their "thou shalt not's" to individuals. In our American ten commandments, the American people issue "thou shalt not's" to their government.

4. We have our major and minor prophecies, the greatest of them all being George Washington's Farewell Address. Both as a foretelling and forthtelling document, that thundering prophecy bears a relation to the American people comparable to the utterances of Isaiah and Jeremiah to the Hebrew people.

5. Our national psalms are not numerous; but in spite of the fact that it is made the butt of ridicule and shallow criticism, *The Star-Spangled Banner* bears a relation to our national feelings not unlike that which the greatest of the psalms of David bore to the feelings of the people who first sang them.

6. The gospel of true Americanism was spoken by the saviour of America. I refer to Abraham Lincoln's Second Inaugural Address. It was good news when first it was uttered: it is good news still.

7. We have our epistles, the greatest of them all being the last article written by Woodrow Wilson. It will endure as long as our present system endures, the vision and the judgment of the man who possessed the clearest insight and the finest analytical mind of any national leader in the history of America.

These seven writings, taken together, constitute what I think might properly be called our *American Canon.* They give us the authoritative rule of the doctrine of Americanism. In describing them we relate our national history. It is my purpose to look at each one briefly; to put it in its historical setting; to meet its author or authors, and to inquire what it is that makes it permanently significant to the American people.

My purpose is to bring to light our vital American ideals in order that we may feel the pull of the formative influences in American history, and know the faith that has made America great; that we may have an intelligent understanding of the progress and toleration in which America has found its spiritual enlargement, and recognize the vision of America as the messiah of nations.

Abraham Lincoln once referred to us as "an almost chosen people." The Constitution of Illinois expresses the conviction that "a frequent recurrence to the fundamental principles of civil government is absolutely necessary to preserve the blessings of liberty."

President Monroe in his Inaugural Address emphasized the importance of an intelligent appreciation of the magnificent social ideal which we call true Americanism when he said: "It is only when the people become ignorant and greedy, when they degenerate into a populace, that they are incapable of exercising their sovereignty. Usurpation is then an easy attainment, and the usurper soon found. The people themselves become a willing instrument of their own debasement and ruin."

With this preparation, let us examine a little more closely *The American Canon.*

CHAPTER I

THE MAYFLOWER COMPACT

THE MAYFLOWER COMPACT is the beginning of American democracy, but for its own beginnings we must look far back of its actual composition. Conditions were being prepared for it through hundreds of years before the Pilgrims left England. The clash of the warfare resulting from the Protestant Reformation was brought to a temporary end by the Peace of Augsburg in 1555. By that Peace, the right of Protestantism to exist was recognized, but unfortunately each state or principality received power to control the creed within its borders. The head of a state was thus able to establish a church and to forbid his subjects to depart from its worship. Henry VIII of England arrogated to himself the sole right to define the faith and control the consciences of his subjects. Some progress away from such arrogant supremacy was made through vicissitudes for a century following. Finally within the Established Church of England there developed a group who were opposed to royal supremacy, and who were in favor of democratizing the Church and purifying the ritual. Hence they were called Puritans. As action and reaction are equal, so the bitterer the persecution of the Puritans by the entrenched High Church party, the more insistent and persistent became the Puritans for reform. The lines of the Puritan movement tightened more and more, so that they came to stand not only for the simplification of the church government and the abolition of empty formalities and disgraceful worldliness, but for a superior sanctity of life. Most of the Puritans were to remain

13

in the Church to purify it, but the more ardent minds among them, despairing of remodeling the Established Church from within, became Separatists.

One of the few small Separatist communities was at Scrooby, a little hamlet in middle England. It was the center of a tenant farming section of a rather poor type. The people had no social distinction. But in 1606 this little group determined to "shake off the yoke of anti-Christian bondage," and "joined themselves, by a Covenant of the Lord, into a Church Estate . . . whatsoever it should cost them, the Lord assisting them."

This little congregation worshiped secretly in Scrooby Manorhouse, the keeper of which was William Brewster, the father of William Brewster, Jr., who later became the famous Elder Brewster of the Pilgrim Colony. From the little village of Austerfield, within walking distance, came the youthful William Bradford, later the great Governor of the Pilgrim Colony.

No sooner were they discovered worshiping in the manorhouse chapel than persecutions began by sanction of the ecclesiastical authorities of Yorkshire. Some, Bradford says, were "taken and clapt up in prison," and others had their "houses besett and watcht night and day and hardly escaped their hands."

By the autumn of 1607 the persecution had become so intolerable that they determined to go to Holland. But the King was equally determined that such emigrations should not take place, and had ordered the ports closed against all who did not have license to go. Thus, as Bradford quaintly remarks, "Though they could not stay, yet they were not suffered to go." Nevertheless, they went, by one means or another, from various ports, a few at a time, suffering all manner of hardships and embarrassments, until, through this

14

winnowing process, more than a hundred men, women, and children were gathered at Amsterdam by August of 1608, "armed with faith and patience."

Amsterdam was a liberal and progressive city; but, because of the general worldliness and presence of many heresies, it proved a disappointing refuge for the Pilgrims. Therefore, within a year, they moved to Leyden, about twenty-two miles southwest of Amsterdam. While they pursued some trades that furnished good training for their future life in Plymouth, yet, for the most part, they were doomed to rude and ill-paid toil. They did not wish their children to become Dutch, nor to be denied an opportunity for education. They disapproved of the defiling encroachments of the world upon the purity of their creed and practice. Hence they determined to seek a new home, where their faith and nationality would remain unimpaired.

After much discussion, they voted to go to America. Financially unable to equip a ship and establish a colony, they sought help from the Virginia Company of London and the Virginia Company of Plymouth. They entered into partnership with the Adventurers to form a voluntary joint-stock company. It was a critical and momentous decision which those Pilgrims made; for trying as was the reality in the New World, psychologically the anticipation of it was worse. They were terrified at the wild stories they had heard of the dangers of shipwreck, the bad sanitation of ships, famine, nakedness, and want. They had been told that the savage Indians flayed men with the shells of fishes, and cut off steaks and chops, which they then broiled upon the coals before the victims' eyes. Bradford states in simple eloquence their brave answer to these objections: "It was answered that all great and honorable actions are accompanied with great difficulties, and must be both enterprised and overcome with answerable courages."

It was evident that only a part of the Church could migrate. So they selected eighty or ninety from among the volunteers, having due regard for age and physical fitness. The whole Church joined in hastening preparations for their departure. Properties were sold, goods donated, money collected. The equipment of tools, foodstuffs, and other supplies displayed good common sense.

The plans called for increasing the original Pilgrim band by recruits from England, with the simultaneous sailing of the Leyden group on the *Speedwell* from Holland and the English group on the *Mayflower* from London. The two groups were to be merged and organized at Southampton, from which port they were to proceed to America with both ships.

One delay followed another, so that it was near the end of July in 1620 before the Leyden Separatists kept their farewell fast, with sermon and the Holy Communion. Bradford writes with the eloquence of restraint: "So they left that goodly and pleasant city which had been their resting place near twelve years; but they knew they were Pilgrims, and looked not much on those things, but lifted up their eyes to the heavens, their dearest country, and quieted their spirits."

The *Mayflower* and *Speedwell* set sail from Southampton on August 15. They had not gone far before the captain of the *Speedwell* said she was unseaworthy, and both ships put in at Dartmouth. Sailing again, another alarm was raised by the captain of the *Speedwell*, and they put in at Plymouth. They ever after believed that the captain and the sailors of the *Speedwell* regretted their agreement, and so crowded the ship with sail that she sprung a leak. At Plymouth, they unloaded the *Speedwell*, transferred much of the cargo to the *Mayflower*, weeded out weak-kneed passengers from both ships, and crowded one hundred and two willing and worthy passengers onto the *Mayflower*. On the 16th of September, 1620, the good ship made her third and final departure —and sailed into immortal renown.

The delays in getting started foredoomed the Pilgrims to land on the bleak New England shore in the midst of winter. They saw the land of England fade from their sight on September 16, and saw no other land until daybreak of November 20. The land which they sighted was Cape Cod. They thought they were headed for the Hudson, considerably to the south of this point. When the captain attempted to steer the *Mayflower* south around Cape Cod, he ran into shoals. On account of the lateness of the season and the roughness of the weather, they turned the ship about and put into Cape Cod harbor (now Provincetown). Here they decided to leave the ship until the more hardy men-folk should explore the neighborhood and find a place suitable for settlement. This meant the definite abandoning of residence within the Virginia Company's territory, under the patent they prized so highly; for they were far to the north of the limits of that patent.

The next day while the ship lay at anchor in Cape Cod Bay, the leaders learned that certain members of the party, especially the recruits secured in London, chafing under restraint, were boldly asserting that as soon as they landed on shore . there would be an end to all authority. For, said they, nobody has authority here—and they were right! The King, it is true, made a general claim to the whole territory; but he had delegated no power to the Pilgrims or to anybody else, not even authorizing them to enter the country.

But the leaders were equal to the emergency. Their decision was swift as lightning. If England had no government for them, they would form a Government of their own. The men of the company were forthwith assembled in the cabin of the *Mayflower;* the situation was frankly explained to them, and then and there the immortal Compact was drawn up and signed by forty-one of the forty-three adult males in the party. Since the two whose names are wanting died soon after, it is likely that they were too sick at the time to sign the Compact.

Of this Compact John Quincy Adams remarked, in 1802: "This is perhaps the only instance in human history of that positive, original social compact which speculative philosophers have imagined as the only legitimate source of government. Here was a unanimous and personal assent by all the individuals of the community to the association, *by which they became a nation.* The settlers of all the former European colonies had contented themselves with the powers conferred upon them by their respective charters, without looking beyond the seal of the royal parchment for the measure of their rights and the rule of their duties. The founders of Plymouth had been impelled by the peculiarities of their situation to examine the subject with deeper and more comprehensive research."

In that Compact were the beginnings of American democracy. It was drafted "in the name of God." The Colony of which it was the instrument of government, was founded "for the glory of God." The Pilgrims covenanted and combined themselves together to enact "just and equal laws," and pledged themselves to yield to these laws "all due submission and obedience."

The first act of the citizens of the new Commonwealth was to confirm John Carver as Governor until their next New Year's Day, which, according to their calendar, fell on March 23.

While the *Mayflower* lay at anchor in Cape Cod Bay, two explorations were made of the Cape. A third coastal exploration, made in the shallop they had brought with them on the

18

Mayflower, took them to Plymouth harbor. On December 21 the exploring party of eighteen men drove their shallop along, looking for a landing place, until they came to the one rock on all that diluvial shore, and on it they landed—the stepping-stone of a nation.

Five days later, the *Mayflower* plowed her way into Plymouth harbor. The loneliness, the anguish, the hardships, the near to starvation, the sickness, the deaths, the sorrows of the Pilgrim band that first winter can scarcely be believed by us. The ravages of what Bradford called the "general sickness" were terrible. Of the one hundred and two Pilgrims who came over on the *Mayflower,* fifty-one—just half the total number—died the first year. Of the twenty-four households, four were completely obliterated by the sickness, and only four households entirely escaped the infection. The devotion with which they served one another during those trying times is beyond all praise.

The mortality left the colony in the hands of young men. Bradford was thirty-one; Winslow, twenty-five; Allerton, thirty-two; Miles Standish, thirty-six, and John Alden, twenty-one.

Carver was re-elected Governor in March, but died shortly after. Thereupon William Bradford was elected Governor. Until his death in 1657 Bradford was the soul of the Colony. He was a truly great man. Concerning him, Cotton Mather wrote: "He was a person for study as well as action: and hence, notwithstanding the difficulties through which he passed in his youth, he attained unto a notable skill in languages. The Dutch tongue was become almost as vernacular to him as the English. The French tongue he could also manage. The Latin and Greek he had mastered. But the Hebrew he most of all studied. Because, he said, he would see with his own eyes the ancient Oracles of God in their native beauty. He was also well skilled in History, in Antiquity, and in Philosophy. . . . But the crown of all was, his holy, prayerful, watchful, and fruitful Walk with God: wherein he was very exemplary."

Not only was he Governor of the Colony for the rest of his life, except for a few brief intervals, but for a while he was secretary and treasurer as well, and at the same time ministered to the sick with his own hands and helped the men as they toiled in the fields.

Terrible as were the sufferings of that first winter at Plymouth, when the *Mayflower* set sail for England in the spring not a single one of the Pilgrims returned with it. Longfellow speaks the word for us:

> "O strong hearts and true! not one went
> back in the *Mayflower!*
> No, not one looked back, who had
> set his hand to this plowing."

They stayed, and lived their own lives in their own way. They stayed, and were loyal to the Compact by which they governed themselves. Under it they held elections; enacted laws; punished law violators; made treaties with the Indians; abolished the communistic scheme with which they had started out; settled their own property question by purchasing the common stock from the Adventurers and distributing the land among the citizens, giving to them titles to private ownership; made Captain Miles Standish head of their military organization, and planted the first permanent independent settlement in the New World, in which the initiative lay with themselves and not with capitalists or kings.

The Mayflower Compact was the fundamental law of their new State. It pointed the way to equal rights and common duties. It is an immortal document, an important contribution to the civic thought of the world. Under it the Pilgrim Colony was not intolerant, nor bigoted, nor overly severe, nor unjust. The Pilgrims applied the Bible to common life in a practical way. They guaranteed religious liberty. They stressed the imperative necessity of righteous character. They exhibited no sickly, simpering sentimentality toward indolence or crime. They had a social conscience that manifested itself in law, the means by which individual conduct was socially controlled. They believed in God with passionate devotion. Their lives were God-centered. God was no mere figure of speech to those sturdy Pilgrim sires.

In spite of the terrible hardships and unspeakable suffering and losses, the Pilgrims stayed in their new home. They stayed because they were able to see the eternal in the temporal, and the invisible in the visible, and because among them the material was dominated by the spiritual.

> "God had sifted three kingdoms to find
> the wheat for this planting,
> Then had sifted the wheat as the living
> seed of a nation;
> So say the chronicles old, and such
> is the faith of the people."

They stayed, because they had found that for which they went in quest when the warning wind sighed in the sails of the old *Mayflower* and they left behind their native land, its history, its throne, its Church, its gold, its worldly cheer, and the green mounds where their brave sires slumbered. The foot of their ship had been set in a pathless sea. They had groped their way through storms and fogs, and mists and blinding rain. They had landed at last on a frozen shore, bleak and dread; but they were so glad that as they knelt in prayer the very snows seemed warm, and the snowflakes on their cheeks melted into tears of gratitude. Pioneers of true

Americanism, they stayed, they conquered, they sowed their seed in the sacred soil of the rights of men, and garnered a goodly harvest.

> "Aye, call it holy ground,
>   The soil where first they trod!
> They have left unstained what there they found—
>   Freedom to worship God!"

CHAPTER II

THE DECLARATION OF INDEPENDENCE

THE DECLARATION OF INDEPENDENCE, our exodus from bondage, came out of a vast and noble courage. It does not take much space to write it, or much time to repeat it; but it was the final crown of many years of political revolution.

The early settlements of America were made from different motives, and by people of varying racial inheritances. But no matter by whom the settlements were originally made, the colonies soon all came into the possession of Great Britain.

As early as 1660 we find the specific beginnings of oppression. The British government passed and attempted to enforce the despised Navigation Acts. Then, in 1760, George III came to the throne. He was young (only twenty-two years old), dull, uneducated, intolerant, bigoted, and, finally, crazy. His mother had dinned into his ears the dictum: "George, be king!" He accepted the then common European idea that a colony existed only to enrich the mother country. He thought he saw in his American possessions a convenient source of revenue to help meet his war debts. Therefore he began through Parliament the collection of new taxes and the enforcement of the Navigation Acts. Commanders of British frigates were given authority to search American homes for smuggled goods.

Oppression followed oppression, insult was heaped upon insult, injustice was added to injustice, until the elemental power of intelligence, character, and feeling in the Americans was ready to burst forth like a volcano. When Patrick Henry cried: "Is life so dear or peace so sweet as to be purchased at the price of chains and slavery?" he simply made articulate the feeling in many an American breast.

A Continental Congress was called in September, 1774, to meet in Philadelphia. The declared purpose of this Congress was: "To consult on the present state of the colonies; and to deliberate upon wise and proper measures for the recovery of their just rights and liberties; and the restoration of union and harmony between Great Britain and the colonies, most ardently desired by all good men."

The colonists at this time were simply standing upon their rights as Englishmen. They sent a petition to the King which the King refused to receive. The second Continental Congress was called to meet in May, 1775, within a month after the battles of Lexington and Concord. The Revolutionary War was now on. The Americans started out to defend their "ancient rights," but soon discovered that there were new rights for them. By the summer of 1776 these new rights were formulated into the Declaration of Independence.

And so we come to the Declaration of Independence—which was a crystallization of the sentiment of the day. Thomas Jefferson, the author of the Declaration, was accused by more than one person of plagiarism in the writing of it. For instance, some forty-four years later a declaration of independence alleged to have been adopted by the citizens of Mecklenburg, North Carolina, came to light. It was the subject of much debate, but my own investigations lead me to pronounce it apocryphal. But many writers were saying things that undoubtedly influenced the thinking of Jefferson. John Dickinson, an influential leader from Pennsylvania, wrote his cogent *Letters From a Farmer in Pennsylvania to the Inhabitants of the British Colonies.* Benjamin Franklin's pragmatic mind marshaled the facts of history and philosophy to the support of his position that Parliamentary legislation for the colonies was "usurpation." Thomas Paine's pamphlet called *Common Sense* exerted almost as great an influence upon the mind of America in 1776 as did Harriet Beecher Stowe's *Uncle Tom's Cabin* in the years preceding the Civil War.

In 1822 John Adams wrote a letter to Pickering, in which he said concerning the Declaration, "There is not an idea in it but what had been hackneyed in Congress for two years before." Adams contended that the "natural rights" philosophy was a commonplace of the day and that the political crimes listed by Jefferson were known to all. In his reply Jefferson did not dispute the fact that the Declaration was a commonplace compilation. This is his answer:

Pickering's observations, and Mr. Adams' in addition, that it contained no new ideas, that it is a commonplace compilation, its sentiments hacknied in Congress for two years before, . . . may all be true. Of that I am not to be the judge. Richard H. Lee charged it as copied from Locke's treatise on Government. . . . I know only that I turned to neither book nor pamphlet while writing it. I did not consider it as any part of my charge to invent new ideas altogether and to offer no sentiment which had ever been expressed before.

If the Declaration had contained things that nobody had thought of before, they probably would not have thought of them again. Congress would never have adopted a declaration of independence that contained either philosophy or history that they did not accept, and that the country as a whole did not accept. Jefferson, by a process of mental evaporation, as it were, gathered up the inarticulate, or half-expressed, beliefs of the day, and precipitated them in cogent and unforgettable phrases in the Declaration of Independence. In writing to Lee, in 1825, Jefferson reaffirmed that he only attempted to express the ideas of the Whigs, who had no disagreement among themselves on the subject.

The truth is that the philosophy of the day might have lain in the public mind as water-soaked logs, had it not been that the British government struck the steel of oppression upon the flint of American sense of freedom that had developed with the development of the country, and the spark struck out kindled the land into a flame with its heat, and the philosophy of the day took fire and blazed up so brightly that it illuminated the whole world.

When we come to the actual writing of the Declaration, we find this entry in the Journal of Congress on Friday, June 7, 1776, in the handwriting of Charles Thomson, the Secretary:

Certain resolutions being moved & seconded Resolved That the consideration of them be referred till to morrow morning & that the members be enjoined to attend punctually at 10 o'clock in order to take the same into consideration.

These "certain resolutions" declared that "these United Colonies are, and of right ought to be, free and independent States."

On June 11, a committee was appointed to prepare the Declaration of Independence. "The members chosen Mr Jefferson, Mr J Adams, Mr Franklin, Mr Shearman & Mr R. R. Livingston." On July 1 discussion of the original motion of independence was renewed. July 2 the final vote was taken, and the resolution was adopted. Thus our independence from Great Britain was voted on July 2, but the Declaration of Independence was not adopted until two days later, July 4.

The man chosen by his fellow committeemen to write the Declaration was Thomas Jefferson, a young man of thirty-three, from Virginia. He was a tall, charming, red-headed lawyer; a horseman, a scientist, a philosopher, a man of wealth and social position, an aristocrat-democrat. He was one of America's truly great men—one of our greatest. Jefferson was chosen to write the Declaration of Independence because, as John Adams said, he had "a reputation for literature, science, and a happy talent of composition. Writings of his were handed about remarkable for the peculiar felicity of expression."

Concerning the actual drafting of the Declaration of Independence, Thomas Jefferson, writing to Madison in 1823, says:

> The Committee of 5 met, no such thing as a sub-committee was proposed, but they unanimously pressed on myself alone to undertake the draught. I consented; I drew it; but before I reported it to the committee I communicated it separately to Dr. Franklin and Mr. Adams requesting their corrections: . . . and you have seen the original paper now in my hands, with the corrections of Dr. Franklin and Mr. Adams interlined in their own handwriting. Their alterations were two or three only, and merely verbal. I then wrote a fair copy, reported it to the committee, and from them, unaltered to the Congress.

Jefferson sat in the parlor of his second-floor lodgings at the corner of Seventh and Market Streets, Philadelphia, and, without consulting a book or pamphlet, wrote in a half day's time our great National Symbol. The rough draft may be seen now in the Library of Congress. There are many corrections in it—words crossed out, and words written in. It is filled with interlining and marginal notes. Most of these emendations are in the handwriting of Jefferson himself.

After Jefferson had written the Declaration, he submitted it to John Adams and Benjamin Franklin. Adams made two corrections, and Franklin, five. It was then submitted to the committee of five, and approved without further change.

Jefferson then made what he calls a "fair copy" to use in making the report to Congress.

Jefferson's draft was reported to Congress on June 28. It was laid on the table until July 1. On that day, it was debated, and adopted by the committee of the whole. Then on the 2d, it will be remembered, the resolution of independence was adopted by Congress, but not the Declaration as drafted by Jefferson. Jefferson's draft was considered again on the 3d of July, and finally adopted on July 4, 1776. It was signed later.

Fifty-six names are appended to this immortal document. They represented every stratum of society, so far as society had become stratified in America at that time. For the most part, the signers were well educated. They were men in the very strength and prime of their manhood. They were neither foolish and radical youth nor old men in their dotage. The average age of the fifty-six signers was 44 years. Samuel Adams was 53 years; John Hancock, 39; R. H. Lee, 44; Benjamin Harrison, 36; John Adams, 40; Thomas Jefferson, 33; Benjamin Franklin, 70; Roger Sherman, 55; R. R. Livingstone, 29.

The effect of the adoption of the Declaration of Independence was instant and epochal. It awakened joy throughout the entire land. It united the Colonies as nothing else could have done. It changed a defensive war for the redress of wrongs into a war for the establishment of a separate government. It drew a clear-cut issue between those who were loyal to the newly formed government and those who were loyal to the British crown. It encouraged the people to endure hardship and privation for the cause of freedom, and prompted the soldiers to plunge with a new and dauntless pride into the crimson sea of carnage.

From 1776 to the present hour the Declaration of Independence has been the inspiration of a new hope among the oppressed of every tribe and nation. Let persons in affluent circumstances try as they will to deny its dictum that "all men are created equal," still the poor and unfortunate and dispossessed will grasp at it as drowning men at a straw. Undoubtedly, what the Fathers of 1776 were trying to say was that under just government all men are equal in political privilege and political obligation. The Declaration tells them that there is but one family picnicking on this right little tight little playground of ours called the earth. Adam, or cave man, or Anthropoidea—it does not matter—the blood of the first man is in all our veins. And the Declaration of Independence is the Call of the Blood.

The Declaration's doctrine that governments derive their just powers from the consent of the governed made for the spread of democracy throughout all the earth. Although at the present time we see the recrudescence of tyranny in the totalitarian State and the dictator, yet wherever and whenever the Declaration's doctrine is accepted, rulers can be no more than attorneys, agents, trustees, and servants of the people.

The principles of the Declaration of Independence have been used to buttress religious toleration as well as political freedom. Charles Carroll, the only Roman Catholic to sign the Declaration, and the last of all the signers to die, wrote, February 20, 1829:

When I signed the Declaration of Independence I had in view not only our independence of England, but the toleration of all sects professing the Christian religion, and communicating to them all equal rights. Happily this wise and salutary measure has taken place for eradicating religious feuds and persecution, and become a useful lesson to all governments.

The Declaration, as originally presented to Congress, contained three references to God: the first in the opening paragraph, where the "laws of nature and of nature's God" are invoked; the second in the second paragraph, where "we hold these truths to be self-evident that all men . . . are endowed by their Creator with inherent and inalienable rights" (which Congress amended to read "certain unalienable rights"); and the third, where the signers appeal "to the Supreme Judge of the world for the rectitude of our intentions." The draft presented to Congress closed with this sentence: "And, for the support of this declaration, we mutually pledge to each other our lives, our fortunes, and our sacred honor." Congress amended this sentence by inserting after the word "declaration" the clause: "with a firm reliance on the protection of Divine Providence."

America is the Messiah of Nations. Her special mission is to furnish hospice for freedom. She must guard the idea of Liberty as the never-sleeping dragon of mythology guarded the garden of the Hesperides. We must make good. But while we live and die for our ideals of democracy we must not forget God.

CHAPTER III

THE CONSTITUTION OF THE UNITED STATES

OUR book of fundamental law is the *Constitution of the United States*. It has now been the fundamental law of America for one hundred and fifty years. It is the oldest written constitution of government in the world, and thus the present form of government of the United States of America is the oldest under any written definition in the whole wide world.

The Constitution is a witness to the self-restraint which the American people of 1787 were wise enough to place upon themselves and their posterity.

The Constitution did not spring Pallas-like from the brain of Jove. It was, rather, the crowning of the toilsome evolution of the ages. All the political strivings of the past from Marathon, where the dauntless soldiers of loyal Greece achieved the liberty of Athens, to Runnymede, where the English barons wrung from a tyrant King the Magna Charta —all these strivings are alive in our republic today. As an instrument for the protection of rights, our Constitution roots in and grows out of the heroic past of the English-speaking people.

The original recommendation for the "convening of a General Congress" was made by Benjamin Franklin in July, 1773. In fulfillment of his suggestion, which had been favorably received by a number of the Colonies, the first Continental Congress met in Philadelphia in September, 1774. It really was not a congress in the sense that it possessed any power. It was merely a conference of delegates from the colonies who came together to discuss the grievances which they had against Great Britain, and to confer about possible methods of redress of those grievances.

The Second Continental Congress met in 1775, but before it met, the Battles of Lexington and Concord had been fought. Relative to historic military engagements, they were the merest skirmishes; but in very truth the shot fired "by the rude bridge that arched the flood" at Concord was "heard round the world." When the sod of Lexington Green soaked in the first blood spilled for American independence, it was as seed that grew and blossomed into the crimson bloom of battle. Nothing else could so effectively have made the colonists all along the Atlantic seaboard recognize the need of united effort as Britain's use of arms against the Americans who up to this time had regarded themselves as British.

From now on until the end of the War the Continental Congress was the one symbol of the political unity of America. But it was an impotent government, even during the Revolution. It was headless. Such success as it had was due to the common fear of the Red Coats and the spirit of co-operation which characterized the American people—and chiefly to the authority of George Washington, not only as Commander in Chief of the Army, but principally because of his dynamic personality and his unimpeachable integrity. So far as Congress was concerned, it possessed no other powers than persuasion to direct the work. The result was pitiable inefficiency.

Articles of Confederation were adopted by Congress in 1781, near the close of the Revolution. The adoption of Articles of Confederation marked a slight advance over the chaos which had previously obtained, but Congress, under the Articles of Confederation, was utterly impotent. The country was still left without an executive head. There really was no such thing as national authority. The most that you could say for the Articles of Confederation was that they constituted a league of sovereign states.

Forces of disintegration were at work from 1783 to 1787. A state of anarchy obtained. Credit was gone. Congress made recommendations to the different states concerning the raising of revenue, and the states treated the recommendations with contempt. Congress issued paper money, and citizens, in derision, plastered the walls of their houses with it. The army demanded pay, and Congress was unable to pay. The army was in rebellion, and a detachment of disgruntled soldiers actually besieged the State House in Philadelphia, where Congress was meeting. Whereupon, Congress fled to Princeton, New Jersey, and then to New York, where it remained until after the Constitutional Convention. Now that the Red Coats were gone, the American Colonies feared each other more than anything else. Insipient rebellions were breaking out. Wiser Americans, like Washington and Franklin, could foresee nothing but increasing disorder. Anarchy shook the land. Lawlessness was rampant. Business was paralyzed. Nothing was sure except disunity among the states.

Then came the great Constitutional Convention, which was convened and carried through in the spirit of the Declaration of Independence. It presented to the world the spectacle of a revolution without bloodshed. It was a change in the program of government accomplished by the wisest leaders in America.

The Convention met in Independence Hall, Philadelphia, on May 25, 1787. Twelve of the thirteen states sent delegates. The absent state was Rhode Island, which was hopelessly and helplessly in the hands of demagogues. The twelve states chose seventy-two of the leading men of the day. The largest number that ever attended, however, was fifty-five, and the number present when the Convention ended was thirty-nine. Benjamin Franklin was the oldest man in the Convention, and one of the greatest men of his generation, or of any generation. George Washington was chosen President of the Convention. Not many nations have any one man to whom they can ascribe the title of founder with as good reason as can the United States of America give that title to George Washington, and no nation ever had a more truly great founder or leader.

One of the younger men of the Convention to whom we are chiefly indebted for our knowledge of its proceedings was James Madison, a political scholar from Virginia. His faithfully kept and carefully preserved report, although not published until after his death, gives us a knowledge of the four months' toil in that Convention which greatly increases our respect for the intelligent patriotism of the members.

Many of the members of the Convention were youngerly men, but they were almost without exception educated and experienced men—men of character, and substance, and social position. No group ever worked in a more unselfish way than the members of that Convention. There was among them no lusting for the limelight. One of their rules of order was absolute secrecy, and the respect that was given to that rule is hard for us to understand in this age of candid cameras, and newspapers, and radios.

The work of the Convention was at no time easy. It was faced with problems that seemed insoluble, and confronted with difficulties that seemed insurmountable. The Constitution itself was the result of compromise between the more radical and more conservative leaders. The main question was, Should the government be a federal government, that is, a mere league of states, or should it be in truth a consolidated union? From the first, there was a conflict of opinion between the large states and the small states, chiefly on the matter of representation in the government: the large and powerful states naturally feeling that representation should be on the basis of population, or of taxable wealth, or both; the small states insisting that there should be equality of representation in the national Congress, the small states having exactly the same representation as the large ones. The former theory rested back upon the philosophy that a new nation was being born; the latter philosophy rested upon the belief that the separate states were sovereign and absolute, and that these sovereign states were to be given equal representation in some sort of a league of sovereign states.

Some of the delegates argued that they were empowered to do nothing more than to revise the Articles of Confederation, while others insisted that their business was to adopt a new Constitution for a new nation.

The debating in the Convention was on high levels, generally characterized by self-effacement. Political principles rather than personal prejudices were, for the most part, given right of way. Once in awhile debate became acrimonious, and once in awhile threats of secession were made. From the beginning it was apparent that a crisis would be reached concerning representation in the national Congress. On July 16 the great compromise was accepted, by which two houses of Congress were provided for: the House of Representatives, in which the states would have representation on the basis of population, and the Senate, in which the states would have equal representation.

Through arduous toil, and in a spirit of give and take, the Convention finally agreed upon the principles which would determine the Congress, the chief executive, and the judiciary Then, on July 26, they recessed until August 6, during which time a Committee on Detail was instructed to whip these principles into practical shape. The report of this Committee on Draft was the Constitution in embryo.

Then for a month following August 6 the Convention meticulously studied every phrase and every word of the draft. Earnest debate ensued. The way those men comported themselves during that convention justifies the appraisement of James Madison, who declared:

Whatever may be the judgment pronounced on the competency of the architects of the Constitution, or whatever may be the destiny of the edifice prepared by them, I feel it a duty to express my profound and solemn conviction, derived from my intimate opportunity of observing and appreciating the views of the Convention, collectively and individually, that there never was an assembly of men, charged with a great and arduous trust, who were more pure in their motives, or more exclusively or anxiously devoted to the object committed to them.

On September 8 the Convention appointed a Committee on Style. It was composed of experts—men who had demonstrated to their fellow members that they possessed unusual powers of comprehension and analysis, and were capable of using English with lucidity and conciseness of expression. The final literary style was probably that of Gouverneur Morris more than of any other. On September 15 the work of drafting was regarded as finished, and the Constitution was ordered engrossed for signing.

Concerning this immortal instrument of government, the late Lord Bryce said:

The Constitution of the United States, including the amendments, may be read aloud in twenty-three minutes. It is about half as long as Saint Paul's Epistle to the Corinthians, and one fourth as long as the Irish Land Act of 1881. History knows few instruments which in so few words lay down equally momentous rules on a vast range of matters of the highest importance and complexity.

THE CONSTITUTION OF THE UNITED STATES

On September 17 the Convention met for the last time. Of the fifty-five who attended the Convention, only thirty-nine were present at the end. No one was enthusiastic over the result. Convictions had been yielded by everyone. Concessions had been made. The Constitution was so much the result of compromise that no member of the Convention felt pride of authorship in it. On the last day Benjamin Franklin pleaded for its support in one of the most cogent and pleasantly witty and impressive speeches of his notable career. In the course of his speech he expressed a judgment which was perhaps typical of the convictions held by most of the members: that the Constitution was not perfect, but that it was the best that could be gotten, and if it should fail of adoption, the country would drift further and further into anarchy and chaos and bloodshed.

On this last day the great Washington made his only speech of the whole Convention, in which he said: "Should the states reject this excellent Constitution, the probability is that an opportunity will never again offer to cancel another in peace—the next will be drawn in blood."

The Constitution was sent to Congress, meeting in New York, in order that that body might recommend it to the states for adoption. It was required that the Constitution should be adopted by Conventions in at least nine of the states before it should become effective.

The ratification of the Constitution was hotly contested. Speaking by and large—and not too accurately—the uneducated and debtor class, the back-country folk and the small business people and farmers were opposed to it, and the educated and substantial people in business and the professions favored it. Nevertheless, there were some great brains and aristocratic leaders against it, and many of the humbler folk were for it. For a year and a half the forensic battle waged. It seemed almost impossible to secure the Constitution's ratification by the necessary nine states. But within eighteen months, eleven of the thirteen states had ratified it, and George Washington was elected first President of the United States of America. Two states, Rhode Island and North Carolina, ratified the Constitution after Washington's inauguration.

The framers of the Constitution sought to state its purpose in the Preamble, succinct, concise, comprehensive:

> We, the people of the United States, in order to form a more perfect Union, establish justice, insure domestic tranquillity, provide for the common defense, promote the general welfare and secure the blessings of liberty to ourselves and our posterity, do ordain and establish this Constitution for the United States of America.

Note that they say "we, the people" do this. With us, that is trite; but with them it was epochal. The great fight was over whether it was thirteen separate, independent and sovereign states that were doing this, or whether it was one new nation. When England signed the Treaty of Peace at the end of the Revolutionary War, she named each one of the thirteen states separately, as sovereign and independent entities. Here the new Constitution is made by the people of the United States of America! One Nation, indivisible!

Notice, also, that "We, the people, ordain and establish this Constitution." It is no temporary expediency. No provision is made for secession of any state that adopts it. This Union is to stand in perpetuity.

John Marshall, greatest of all Chief Justices of the Supreme Court, stated the political philosophy of the Constitution by declaring that "The government of the United States has been emphatically termed a government of laws, and not of men." The Constitution itself, however, is not so much a code of laws as a charter granted by the people to the Federal government. It was established to protect the people against aggression from without and injustice within. It is the norm or standard by which all laws must be tested. It points plainly to the American principle that just governments obtain their authority from the consent of the governed; that governments are the servants and not the masters of the people. It lays down rules for the control of the government and governmental agencies.

It has been pointed out that there are four basic principles of the Constitution. The first is representative government. That is, legislation is not by the people directly, but by the chosen representatives of the people.

The second and most novel principle of the Constitution is its dual form of government. Under it, the American people are citizens of their respective states in matters reserved to the states, while at the same time they are citizens of the central government, and therefore cease to be citizens of the several states in the sphere of government delegated to the central power. Thus the people are free to make their own laws in their various states, but those laws must not be out of harmony with the principles of the Constitution of the United States.

The third principle is the guaranty of individual liberty through constitutional limitations.

The fourth principle is that of an independent judiciary. This is closely allied to the doctrine of limited governmental powers. This independent judiciary is really the balance wheel of the Constitution. Its importance is not overstated by William Wirt: "If the Judiciary be struck from the system, what is there of any value that will remain; for government cannot subsist without it? It would be as rational to talk of a solar system without a sun."

The framers of the Constitution ransacked history for models and hints and suggestions and help of every kind in the work which they were doing. They found nowhere in history any instrument of government which they could copy. There was one thing, however, which they had learned from history, and that was that in order to preserve freedom under any form of government, the powers of government had to be divided and balanced, so that every person connected with the government would be effectually checked and restrained by others. In 1787, John Adams wrote: "If there is one certain truth to be collected from the history of all ages, it is this: That the people's rights and liberties, and the democratic mixture in a constitution, can never be preserved without a strong executive, or, in other words, without separating the executive power from the legislature."

Thus the President's powers are checked by Congress, and Congress's powers are checked by the President, and each one is held within the strict limitations of the Constitution by the Supreme Court.

The Constitution makes provision for its own amendment. The method is difficult enough to make rash and reckless schemes run the gantlet of time and scrutiny, and yet it is sufficiently easy of accomplishment that any provision which really needs amendment can have it without much delay. Since our government was organized, there have been more than thirty-two hundred amendments proposed by congressmen. Up to date, a total of twenty-one amendments have been adopted—but since the twenty-first amendment repeals the eighteenth, it means that nineteen amendments now stand as a part of the Constitution.

The first ten amendments really constitute our Bill of Rights. It was necessary for the proponents of the Constitution to promise the adoption of this Bill of Rights in order to secure the ratification of the Constitution. The purpose was to safeguard rights and immunities which we had inherited from our ancestors.

The first article specifically sets forth the four fundamental freedoms: "Congress," it reads, "shall make no law respecting an establishment of religion or prohibiting the free exercise thereof; or abridging the freedom of speech or of the press; or the right of the people peaceably to assemble and to petition the government for a redress of grievances."

Thence the document goes on to list and to specify personal rights. "The right of the people to keep and bear arms shall not be infringed. . . . No soldier shall, in time of peace, be quartered in any house without the consent of the owner, nor in war time, but in a manner to be prescribed by law. . . . The right of the people to be secure in their persons, houses, papers and effects, against unreasonable searches and seizures, shall not be violated."

The right of free men to trial and justice is specified: "No person shall be held to answer for a capital or other infamous crime unless on presentment or indictment of a grand jury. . . . Nor be deprived of life, liberty, or property without due process of the law; nor shall private property be taken for public use without just compensation. . . . The accused shall enjoy the right to a speedy and public trial by an impartial jury. . . . No fact tried by a jury shall be otherwise re-examined in any court of the United States than according to the rules of common law. . . . Excessive bail shall not be required, nor excessive fines imposed, nor cruel and unusual punishments inflicted. . . ."

The last two articles of our Bill of Rights take care to specify that in so enumerating certain rights there is no denial or disparagement of others retained by the people, and to make it clear that powers not specifically delegated to the

41

national government are reserved to the states and to the people.

This Bill of Rights, a definite and integral part of our Constitution—our modern American counterpart of the Mosaic Ten Commandments—is one of our most precious possessions. In dictator countries the masses allow the radio and the press to become instruments of self-delusion. In dictator countries men and women are persecuted because of their religious faith. In dictator countries there is no such thing as free speech or freedom of assembly. Instead, there is intolerance, and bigotry, and persecution. The liberties protected by our Constitution should make us all fight for the preservation of free speech and freedom of worship; for wherever they are denied to one bloc of a country's population, they will sooner or later be denied to another. The great Frenchman, Voltaire, said to an opponent, "I hate and detest what you say, but I will defend, with my life if need be, your right to say it."

John Milton, the English poet, gave expression to a sentiment that we sometimes seem not to prize simply because it is guaranteed to us by our Constitution. Said Milton, "Give me the liberty to know, to utter, and to argue freely, according to conscience—above all liberties."

This free speech provision of our Bill of Rights is the safety valve upon the engine of our democracy. Tie down the safety valve, and you may have an explosion that will ruin the whole engine. Experience and common sense dictate that we should keep in good condition the safety valve that gives opportunity for the blowing off of excess steam.

All those who love the Constitution—who love it intelligently—will vow with Thomas Jefferson, who, when he was President, wrote, "I have sworn upon the altar of God eternal hostility against every form of tyranny over the mind of man."

THE CONSTITUTION OF THE UNITED STATES

The American Canon would be incomplete without the Constitution of the United States. The Constitution has endured because it is worthy to endure. Bess Streeter Aldrich, in her *Song of Years* (1939), makes a prominent citizen say, "The American Constitution, like one of those wondrous rocking stones reared by the Druids, which the finger of a child might vibrate to its center, yet the might of an army could not move from its place—the Constitution is so nicely poised that it seems to sway with every breath of passion, yet so firmly based in the hearts and affections of the people that the wildest storms of treason and fanaticism break over it."

At the end of the Convention in which the Constitution was adopted, George Washington said, "We have raised a standard to which the good and wise can repair; the event is in the hands of God."

In the midst of the Convention, at the time of its greatest crisis, when it seemed as though the Convention were doomed to failure, Benjamin Franklin made one of the greatest speeches of his distinguished lifetime, in which he spoke of the apparent inability of the Convention to solve the problems confronting it, and stated his faith in an overruling Providence and in the power of prayer, and then said:

I have lived, sir, a long time, and the longer I live, the more convincing proofs I see of this truth: That *God governs in the affairs of men*. And if a sparrow cannot fall to the ground without His notice, is it probable that an empire can rise without His aid?

We have been assured, sir, in the sacred writings, that "except the Lord build the House they labor in vain that build it." I firmly believe this; and I also believe that without His concurring aid we shall succeed in this political building no better than the builders of Babel. We shall be divided by our little partial local interests; our projects will be confounded, and we ourselves shall become a reproach and byword down to future ages. And, what is worse, mankind may hereafter from this unfortunate instance,

43

despair of establishing governments by human wisdom and leave it to chance, war, and conquest.

I therefore beg leave to move that henceforth prayers imploring the assistance of Heaven, and its blessings on our deliberations, be held in this Assembly every morning before we proceed to business, and that one or more of the clergy of this city be requested to officiate in that service.

The records do not agree as to what the Convention finally did with Franklin's motion. Madison, who reports it, would indicate that nothing was done about it; but a younger member, Dayton, who also reports it, says that it was acted on favorably by the Convention.

But regardless of what action the Convention took, one thing is certain: if we would prize our religious rights, we ought to use them! Calvin Coolidge said that the founding Fathers of the American republic got their ideas more from the meetinghouse than anywhere else.

The French historian, Guizot, once asked James Russell Lowell, "How long will the American republic endure?"

Lowell replied, "As long as the ideas of the men who founded it continue dominant."

CHAPTER IV

GEORGE WASHINGTON'S FAREWELL ADDRESS

OUR major American prophet is George Washington, and his greatest prophecy is his *Farewell Address*. In popular thought, a prophet is one who foretells, but a more important function of the prophet is to forthtell—and forthtelling includes moral teaching by warning, consoling, exhorting, giving an example of the thing talked about. In that somewhat limited sense, George Washington was a major prophet, and his Farewell Address fixed the standards of American patriotism.

Washington was a man sent of God. He possessed all the essential qualities for the dynamic leadership required of one called to his exalted position. He was well born. He had a strong physique—tall, rugged, clear-eyed, a mighty man with body and limbs of iron. He was a man of great dignity, carrying in his very presence that something that we call authority. The training which he received as a soldier, added to his native abilities, made him one of the greatest military strategists of all time. His courage was sublime, covering the whole range of physical courage, military courage, and moral courage. He knew no fear. He saw the right instinctively, and chose it just as instinctively. He never turned from duty's path, no matter where that path might lead.

Weems's *Life of Washington*, and America's hero worship of him, prompted certain persons in these later years to overwork the debunking of his history. But when the debunkers have done their worst, George Washington still stands forth as our greatest American. His personal character was never impeached nor his reputation sullied. His patriotism should not be unapproachable, but it has not yet been approached by any other. At the time of the American Revolutionary War he was, with one possible exception, the richest man in America. He might have gone to England, and been lionized and feted. He had everything to lose and nothing to gain by espousing the uncertain cause of the colonists. But without reserve he threw his lot in with his fellow Americans. He served through all the awful years of the American Revolution, as the Commander in Chief of the Army, without taking a single cent of pay for his services, and a part of the time paying the ragged American soldiers out of his own pocket. He longed for the comforts of his Mount Vernon home, but during all those years of the Revolution he only once visited Mount Vernon, and that for only a few hours when on a military trip from the North to the South. When the War ended he repaired to his Mount Vernon estate. He loved the delights of country life—the growing of flowers, the designing of hedge-bordered paths, the arranging for the rotation of crops, the fellowship with his simple neighbors, the encouragement of the work of the local church. He sought no honors for himself. He was truly modest. He did not possess that mock modesty which some affect, and which is nothing more than inverted pride. Some of his compatriots honestly believed it was best for the country to establish a monarchy, and they tried to persuade Washington to become king. We in our day make loud profession of democracy, but we show ourselves rather silly in adulation of royal titles. Washington had a chance to be king, and refused even to consider the proposal.

But when anarchy stalked through the land; when it became evident that the Colonies which had been held together during the Revolution by fear of the Red Coats now feared each other more than anything else; when it was easy to foresee that thirteen jarring nations were to be established where these thirteen Colonies had been, then Washington answered the call of duty, and went to Philadelphia to become President of the Constitutional Convention. He attended every session of that Convention from the day it opened on May 25, 1787, until it adjourned on September 17, following.

He again went back to Mount Vernon to rest, speaking modestly of having grown old in the service of his country, and of his eyesight having grown dim in its service too; back to Mount Vernon—this virile, silent man—to dream, perchance, of Boston, Trenton, Valley Forge, Monmouth, and Yorktown. Then he heard his country calling him to be its first President under the Constitution. Lured not by the honors, but by the call of duty, he entered that path of service also.

The first years were bound to be the most severely testing years of the Constitution. Some critics of the Constitution felt that it gave the President too much power, and others felt it did not give him enough. Too much power would end in monarchy, and too much liberty would end in anarchy. The supreme need was a President with the mental powers to appreciate the value of each principle, and with force enough to compel its recognition. Washington, with his tremendous mastery of men, was the man of destiny for that hour. He was President from April 30, 1789, until March 4, 1797.

Those eight years were filled with precedent-making responsibilities. It thrills one to read the history of Washington's administration and see how he, with the unerring instinct of a bird of flight, went straight to the heart of every problem, and solved it in a way that stands the test even to this hour.

Toward the end of his administration, however, rival parties were beginning to find fault and to criticize. Personal ambition and lust for political preferment, and sometimes conscientious political philosophy like that held by Thomas Jefferson, made Washington's heavy burden heavier still, and threw difficulties into the steep road that he was climbing. Therefore, in the fall of 1796, as the time for the election of a President approached, Washington decided to tell his fellow countrymen that he would not stand for election to a third term. There is good reason to conclude that Washington believed that it was better for the country that one man should not hold power for too long a time. At any rate, he gave the example that nobody has ever yet been able to break down —that no one person should be President for a longer period than two terms. In reaching this conclusion he decided to issue what he called his Farewell Address to the American people.

For many years after it was issued, all sorts of charges of plagiarism were made against Washington, it being declared that the address had actually been written by Alexander Hamilton. It is no longer the subject of critical comment, for historical research has revealed the facts in the case. Washington was in the habit of seeking the assistance of his colleagues constantly and intimately in every matter he handled. When they were present with him, he asked for it; when they were absent, he sought their advice by letter. It is a matter of common knowledge to historians that he received help from his most trusted associates in the preparation of many of his great state papers. In the case of the Farewell Address: When Washington decided to deliver this address, he wrote a rough draft of what he had in mind, and sent it to Alexander Hamilton, with the request that Hamilton should return it with any suggestions for its improvement. In reply, Hamilton sent to Washington an enlargement of that draft, together with an alternative suggestion. Washington took these and studied them, recast them in his own words, and sent them back again to Hamilton. This sort of thing went on between the two for some time. But to all intents and purposes, the Address was Washington's. It contained nothing except what he wanted to say; it said what he wanted to say, and, to a large extent, it said it in Washington's actual language. Let us therefore not be sidetracked from our main purpose. However much Hamilton contributed to the writing of the Address, it was remolded by Washington and expressed his ideas.

What are those ideas? It is as though it were the last will and testament of the Father of his Country to his country, and it is a bequest of sagacious advice.

One single exhortation of Washington's has been so oft quoted, and so bandied about by politicians, that many persons think that the whole of Washington's Farewell Address was a warning against entangling alliances—a warning that should keep us out of the League of Nations and the World Court.

As a matter of fact, the isolationists badly err in this use of his Address. What did Washington say? Answer:

Observe good faith and justice towards all nations; cultivate peace and harmony with all. Religion and morality enjoin this conduct; and can it be that good policy does not equally enjoin it? It will be worthy of a free, enlightened, and at no distant period a great nation, to give to mankind the magnanimous and too novel example of a people always guided by an exalted justice and benevolence. . . .

In the execution of such a plan, nothing is more essential than that permanent, inveterate antipathies against particular nations, and passionate attachments for others should be excluded; and that in place of them just and amicable feelings towards all should be cultivated.

That is the context for his advice not to "entangle our

peace and prosperity in the toils of European ambition, rival-ship, interest, humor, or caprice," and against "permanent alliances with any portion of the foreign world," and this in order that we might "choose peace or war, as our interest, guided by justice, shall counsel."

Washington was not an isolationist. He sent commissioners abroad to negotiate treaties of commerce. He advised faithful performance of treaties made. His reason for the advice against "permanent alliances" was in order "to gain time to our country to settle and mature its yet recent institutions." Washington did not advise aloofness: he advised harmony. He counseled "harmony, liberal intercourse with all nations," as "recommended by policy, humanity, and interest." The foreign relationships that Washington really protested against were "antipathies" or "attachments" for "particular nations." He warned against a sycophantic and servile attitude toward any one nation, and at the same time he warned against bait-ing and irritating any one nation. He pleaded that we should not grant "exclusive favors or preferences," but that in our commercial policy we "should hold an equal and impartial hand."

But this advice concerning our relation to foreign countries was only one item in Washington's great prophetic utterance. Let us look at some of the other things he said.

He pleaded "like an angel trumpet-tongued against the deep damnation" of disunion. The unity of government which constituted the people of all the American states one people is, he insisted, a main pillar in the edifice of our real independence. He cogently argued against anything that would mar that essential unity that was provided for in the Constitution of the United States. He urged Americans to accustom themselves to think and speak of the Constitution as of the palladium of their political safety and prosperity.

He therefore warned against anything that would make for disunion; against geographical discriminations and sectional jealousies; against disrespect for the authority of the Union; against obstructions to the execution of the laws enacted under the Constitution; against lawlessness of every kind. Speaking of the government, he said: "Respect for its authority, compliance with its laws, acquiescence in its measures are duties enjoined by the fundamental maxims of true liberty. . . . The very idea of the power and the right of the people to establish government presupposes the duty of every individual to obey the established government."

He counseled against the spirit of innovation which would alter and thus impair the energy of the federal system. He argued for a vigorous protection of that provision of the Constitution which distributes and adjusts the powers of government. He proclaimed against selfish partisanship, pointing out that the "domination of one faction over another, sharpened by the spirit of revenge . . . is itself a frightful despotism." He forever makes plain that when men grow tired of disorders and miseries, and seek to find security and repose in the absolute power of an individual, sooner or later "the chief of some prevailing faction, more able or more fortunate than his competitors, turns this disposition to the purpose of his own elevation, on the ruins of public liberty."

Again he declares that the members of the government— the President, the congressmen, and others—should confine their activities to the spheres permitted by the Constitution, not allowing the powers of one department to encroach upon another. "The spirit of encroachment," he says, "tends to consolidate the powers of all the departments into one, and thus to create, whatever the form of government, a real despotism." If there is anything wrong with the distribution of constitutional powers, "let it be corrected by an amendment in the way which the Constitution designates. But let there be no change by usurpation."

Further along in the Address, Washington says: "As a very important source of strength and security, cherish public credit." He thinks this is extremely important, and advises that in time of peace we should not add to our public debts, but should "discharge the debts which unavoidable wars may have occasioned, not ungenerously throwing upon posterity the burden which we ourselves ought to bear."

In this prophetic utterance, the Father of our Country calls attention to the fact that "virtue or morality is a necessary spring of popular government." To this end, he asks that "institutions for the general diffusion of knowledge" be promoted. Washington was always pleading for higher education. In his will he gave some money to one educational institution, and left other money for the establishment of a national university. The person who would give heed to George Washington's Farewell Address will support our colleges and universities, for Washington said nothing in the whole Address more emphatically than this: "Promote, then, as an object of primary importance, institutions for the general diffusion of knowledge."

In this Address, which he described as the "counsels of an old and affectionate friend," Washington did not speak of many things as "indispensable," but he did speak of one. He said: "Of all the dispositions and habits which lead to political prosperity, religion and morality are indispensable supports." He then goes on to impeach the patriotism of the man who would labor "to subvert these great pillars of human happiness, these firmest props of the duties of men and citizens." He opines that neither property, nor reputation, nor life is secure when people are not sincerely religious. In this emphasis upon religion George Washington's life squared

52

with his words. He was a deeply religious man. He was a regular attendant at and faithful supporter of the Church. He had a firm faith in God and in the life hereafter. He believed in the efficacy of prayer and in the overruling providence of God.

Such is the prophecy of our major prophet, George Washington. His life was not dependent on praise or disturbed by fame. He did not think more highly of himself than he ought to think. He met the duties of the day with a resolute serenity. His religious faith was the source and inspiration of his noble life. The Duke of Wellington pronounced him "the purest and noblest character of modern times." Abraham Lincoln declared that "Washington is the mightiest name of earth—long since mightiest in the cause of civil liberty; still mightiest in moral reformation. On that name no eulogy is expected."

CHAPTER V

"THE STAR-SPANGLED BANNER"

NATIONAL songs are born of fervent patriotism. The song of Deborah, the psalm of Moses, and many of the psalms of David reveal a passionate patriotism. The same principle holds true for every people and every age.

America also has her national songs. Different ones have risen to popular favor at different times. The Revolutionary soldiers marched to the tune of "Yankee Doodle," sounded forth on the shrill call of the fife and the roll of the drum. In succeeding generations, we find Americans singing "My Country, 'Tis of Thee," or "Hail Columbia," or "The Battle Hymn of the Republic," or "America the Beautiful," and from time to time, many others. Nothing sets the ephemeral in contrast with the permanently valuable more strikingly than national songs.

The one song that for nearly a century and a quarter has claimed the attention of Americans in patriotic mood is "The Star-Spangled Banner." It is now officially our national anthem, and is the only song that has ever been declared by Congress to be our national anthem. I therefore pick it out as our one national song that has stood the canonical test for inclusion in *The American Canon.*

"If I may write the songs of a people," said Fletcher of Saltoun, "I care not who writes its laws." What Fletcher meant to say was that the behavior of any people is as much determined by sentiment as by legislation. As an eagle rises on two wings, so society is borne onward and upward equally by reason and affection.

Shelley says that "Poets are the hierophants of unappreciated inspiration; the mirrors of the gigantic shadows which futurity casts upon the present." Possessors of this spirit of song are all one tribe, whether they be harpers among the herdsmen, prophets in the presence of kings, minstrels or troubadours, ballad peddlers or poet laureates. They are a tribe to which is bequeathed the honor and glory of preserving whatever is fine and worth while in the spirit of the times.

Critics say that Francis Scott Key, the author of "The Star-Spangled Banner," was not a poet. I do not know that anybody will argue with the critics about this. Let us concede at once that he was not a poet. But it has happened in more than one instance that a man who is not a poet in a professional or technical sense has written some one great poem. That is the case here. Francis Scott Key was not a poet, but "The Star-Spangled Banner," which he wrote, stands the test of poetry. By profession, he was a lawyer who lived in Frederick, Maryland. At the time that he composed "The Star-Spangled Banner" he was in the United States Army in the second war with Great Britain—the War of 1812-14.

A Dr. William Beanes had been captured by the British soldiers and made a prisoner of war on board the British fleet. Francis Scott Key was one of Doctor Beanes's intimate friends. At the same time he was a brother-in-law of Chief Justice Taney of the United States Supreme Court. Through Chief Justice Taney's influence, Mr. Key secured permission from President Madison to go on the British fleet, under a flag of truce, to secure the release of Doctor Beanes, if possible. Key was accompanied by John S. Skinner, governmental agent for flags of truce and exchange of prisoners. Key and Skinner were treated kindly by the British officers, but were detained on board the British fleet until after the fleet should make its attack upon Baltimore.

It was on the night of September 13, 1814, that the British fleet bombarded Fort McHenry. Key and Skinner and Doctor Beanes spent the night on the deck of the vessel upon which they were detained. Key told about it afterward. He said that every time a shell was fired, they watched it until it exploded. They noted also the returning fire from the Fort. They knew that as long as the Fort returned the fire, it had not surrendered. By the light of "the rocket's red glare" and "the bombs bursting in air," they could see that the American flag still waved over Fort McHenry.

A short time before dawn the firing ceased, and with it came a period of awful suspense. Key did not know but that the Fort had been captured, which meant the surrender of Baltimore to the British. But "by the dawn's early light," they saw that "our flag was still there." In the high emotional condition of the moment, the song came to him. He jotted down upon the back of a letter the clauses and phrases and lines as they came to him. During the day he and his companions were released. That night, in a hotel, he wrote the song out as it stands today. He used the meter of a song that was popular at that time, and set his new song to be sung to that same then popular tune, "Anacreon in Heaven."

The next morning he showed his song to Judge Nicholson, who said that he liked it. It was then sent to a printer, and copies were struck off in the form of handbills. At first, on Judge Nicholson's suggestion, the song was called "The Defense of Fort McHenry." The following January 6 (just before the greatest battle of the War of 1812-14—the Battle of New Orleans), the song was given its present title—"The Star-Spangled Banner."

It is the only official national anthem we have ever had,

and it was not so constituted until 1931. Prior to that time it had been used along with "America," and "Hail Columbia," and "Yankee Doodle," and "Marching Through Georgia" on patriotic occasions. But when Mr. Jefferson Levy introduced a bill into Congress on January 30, 1913, to make "The Star-Spangled Banner" our national anthem, the bill was referred to the Judiciary Committee, and died there.

Its first official recognition came in 1916, when President Woodrow Wilson, in answer to a Departmental demand for a song for State occasions, designated "The Star-Spangled Banner." That gave it a place during the World War and following that was not accorded to any other American air. Then on March 3, 1931, the United States Congress adopted a bill making "The Star-Spangled Banner" our official national anthem.

No other writing in the collection which I am calling THE AMERICAN CANON has had to stand up against such criticism as has "The Star-Spangled Banner." It is perennially attacked, sometimes because it is said that the tune is unsingable, but more often by persons who honestly think that it is not expressive of the American spirit at its best. They attack it because they say it fosters a spirit of militarism and of narrow nationalism.

Let us look at it in the light of these criticisms. Nationalism may be either a good thing or a bad thing. Nationalism that is aggressive and bellicose is to be condemned. It results both from feelings of superiority and from feelings of inferiority; the superior strutting because they are victors, and the inferior blustering because they have been vanquished. Nationalism that is selfish, and self-centered, and wrapped in the cloak of self-interest is self-defeating. Nationalism that rides rough-shod over the rights of weak nations, that menacingly carries a "big stick," that struts and blusters and dares others, that arrogantly takes by force and violence what it wants from another—such nationalism menaces the peace of the world, and is bad and only bad. Nationalism, more commonly called patriotism, that makes a fetish of the symbols of government, and that prates the adolescent lie, "my country, right or wrong"—that kind of patriotism is what Samuel Johnson had in mind when he declared it to be "the last refuge of a scoundrel."

But rightly understood, patriotism is one of the noblest sentiments and one of the most sovereign instincts of a good man. The absence of it indicates a dead soul, as Sir Walter Scott suggests in the "Lay of the Last Minstrel":

> "Breathes there the man with soul so dead
> Who never to himself hath said,
> This is my own, my native land?"

To Scott's idea we hasten to add the patriotism of the prophets of Israel. Patriotism meant to them more than an emotional thrill. They had the sentiment: their longing for Jerusalem when exiled, and their joy at the sight of the Holy City, as set forth in the Psalms, bear witness to the fervency of their affection for their country. But their patriotism was also shot through with an ethical passion. They proved their patriotism by denouncing the sins which, like dry rot, ate the very life out of their nation.

There is nothing in "The Star-Spangled Banner" which can be invoked in favor of a narrow nationalism as against the higher patriotism of world brotherhood. On Commonwealth Avenue in Boston is an impressive statue of William Lloyd Garrison, inscribed with one of his own immortal utterances: "My country is the world. My countrymen are humankind." That is Christian patriotism. It accepts the

58

spirit of Christ's Sermon on the Mount as the Magna Charta of our own nation, and the spirit of the good Samaritan as the guiding principle in the neighborhood of nations.

That which is vital and intelligent in patriotism comes not from an exclusive love of one's own country, but from self-forgetfulness in the possession of a larger idea of humanity. If the triumph of patriotism means the discomfiture of other nations, the quenching of their aspirations, then patriotism is only tyranny on a larger scale.

Unless a man loves something higher than national conceit of superiority and material advantage, he cannot love his country wisely and worthily. The true patriot must love his country as he loves himself: that is, he must love truth and justice most, seeking these for himself and his country at the cost of lower and passing interests. "Righteousness exalteth a nation: but sin is a reproach to any people."

The patriotism of a mature mind requires us to raise a race of patriots who will have no more of that sophomoric toast of Stephen Decatur's: "Our country! In her intercourse with foreign nations may she always be in the right; but our country, right or wrong." A true patriot will be ready to die for his country, if need be, when his country is right; and he will be just as ready to die to make his country right, if need be, when his country is wrong. We honor the person who dies for his country. It is meet and right that we should. But the person who makes his country worth dying for is equally worthy of honor.

America must show the way to international co-operation and good will. We must not allow the spirit of greed and selfishness and ambition to find rootage in the soil of this continent. America gave to the world a new democracy for man. She now may give to the world a democracy of nations.

With the foregoing thoughts in mind, let us look at "The

Star-Spangled Banner" and see whether it deserves the harsh things frequently said about it by its critics.

While, of course, it is full of the imagery of battle, it is not the battle that is glorified: it is the flag that is still seen in spite of the battle. Nowhere in the song is there a glorifying of war for war's own sake, or of war as a national policy for national aggrandizement. The person who sees nothing but the "rocket's red glare," and the "bombs bursting in air," and the "foe's haughty host," has missed the whole point of the song. The feeling that surges through it is created by the sight of the flag! It is the banner that is loved, not war.

It may not be out of place to observe that the United States flag is a beautiful flag. This judgment is not necessarily inspired by sentimental regard for the nation which it symbolizes. From an aesthetic point of view, the design of the flag, its geometrical proportions and the arrangement of its colors constitute it probably the most beautiful banner in the world. Of course the flag is only a piece of bunting or of silk that once lay upon the floor of a warehouse. It is significant because it is the sign of the American government. But one does not need to pass from the thing signified to the sign and become an idolater of the flag to feel a swift response to the beauty of it.

The flag came into existence almost a year after the Declaration of Independence was adopted. It was on June 14, 1777, that the Continental Congress voted that the flag of the United States of America should consist of thirteen red and white stripes and a union of blue with thirteen stars. Previously, flags of various designs had been used by the army and by the several states. For awhile a stripe and a star were added for each new state admitted to the Union. But before long, Congress ordained that the flag should consist of the thirteen stripes of alternate red and white, representing the original thirteen states, and that in the little square heaven of blue there should be one star for each state in the Union. Thus the flag at present has the thirteen stripes and forty-eight stars— the most glorious constellation in the firmament of nations.

There is a philosophy of colors. The particular shade of red in our Star-Spangled Banner is scarlet. It is a bright, brilliant red, of orange tinge. Thus the red of love and courage and passion plus the tinge of orange which stands for benevolence gives us the scarlet of the Feast of Martyrs—and of the Star-Spangled Banner. Red represents blood, and blood represents fire, and blood and fire are life.

White is the harmonious blending of all the hues and colors and beauties of light. White without any mixture of darkness sets forth the pure absolute triumph of light. The writer of the Apocalypse tells us that the redeemed are "arrayed in white robes," and then, as though he were afraid we might not understand his symbolism, he hastens on to say that the white robes are the righteous acts of the saints. It is no fictitious righteousness. It is the result of work and sacrifice: we are told that they themselves "have washed their robes and made them white in the blood of the Lamb."

Thus American patriotism as symbolized in our national emblem aims at character that is not only spotless but also complete—the combination of all virtues, the balancing of all excellences, a display of all the beauties of grace.

The white stars are set in a square of blue. Since blue is the color of the zenith of the clear sky, it early came to be associated with heaven, and therefore was regarded as sacred. Blue is the color that traditionally symbolizes virtue. Virtue is integrity of character; moral behavior; conformity to the standards of right. It is honesty that goes beyond the requirements of mere "legal honesty." Hence the blue in our flag may be made to stand for that quality of pure patriotism that characterized the signers of the Declaration of Independence and of the Constitution of the United States, and the other makers of our *American Canon*.

Stars stand not only for the states of the Union: they stand for ideals and aspirations—the aspirations of a free people and the ideals of democracy. Our flag is a constant summons to Americans to follow the star toward perfection even as the wise men of old followed the star that led them to the Bethlehem manger.

Our national anthem, "The Star-Spangled Banner," glorifies the flag not only because its stripes are stroked in ripples of white and of red, and not merely because its white stars laugh down their delightful light from their little square heaven of blue, but chiefly because the flag is the symbol of the rights guaranteed to us by the Declaration of Independence and the Constitution of the United States; because it is a pledge of liberty and justice, a sign that the rights of the weakest will be respected wherever it floats.

Note particularly the last stanza of our national anthem, and see how strikingly in harmony it is with the main drift of *The American Canon:*

"Oh! thus be it ever when freemen shall stand
    Between their loved homes and war's desolation!
Blest with victory and peace, may the heaven-rescued land
    Praise the Power that hath made and preserved us a nation!
Then conquer we must, when our cause it is just,
And this be our motto: 'In God is our Trust.'
    And the Star-spangled Banner in triumph shall wave
    O'er the land of the free and the home of the brave."

The spirit of our national anthem is one with the spirit of the Declaration of Independence. It was conceived in the same teachings. And what were those teachings? President Calvin Coolidge, in his address at Philadelphia, at the celebration of the one hundred and fiftieth anniversary of the signing of the Declaration of Independence, pronounced the inescapable—"The conclusion that in its great outlines the Declaration of Independence was the result of the religious teachings of the preceding period." He had made extended research, which clearly showed that the intellectual life of our forefathers "centered around the meetinghouse. They were intent upon religious worship. . . . They were a people who came under the influence of a great spiritual development and acquired a great moral power. No other theory is adequate to explain or comprehend the Declaration of Independence. It is the product of the spiritual insight of the people. . . . The things of the spirit come first. . . . We must follow the spiritual and moral leadership which they showed."

So spoke Calvin Coolidge, and that is the contention and the exhortation of *The Star-Spangled Banner.* We can conquer only "when our cause it is just." We can feel secure in our national safety only so long as we practice our national motto: "In God is our Trust."

CHAPTER VI

ABRAHAM LINCOLN'S SECOND INAUGURAL ADDRESS

T HE gospel of Americanism *par excellence* is *Abraham Lincoln's Second Inaugural Address*. By every measurement, it is good news, glad tidings. It was spoken by the man who, more than any other, merits the appellation, "saviour of the American Union."

Slavery was a vexatious question from the beginning of our national history until it was ended in the shock of Civil War. Some of the most eloquent passages in the Declaration of Independence as originally written by Thomas Jefferson inveighed against the enslavement of the Negro people. Jefferson writhed as he saw the Continental Congress, under the lash of the Southern constituency, cut those eloquent passages out of the Declaration. The same question came to the front again in the Constitutional Convention, and it was a live issue—alive in increasing bitterness of feeling and peril for the safety of the Union—down to the days of the Civil War.

Abraham Lincoln, thanks partly to his superb abilities, partly to the trust his fellow men had in him, and partly to the overruling providence of God—Abraham Lincoln became the instrument for striking the shackles off the wrists of the slaves. Lincoln's arguments were based almost exclusively upon philosophy learned in two documents: One was the New Testament, and the other was the Declaration of Independence. He unequivocally declared that all his political philosophy could be traced to the Declaration of Independence. It was his application of the principles enunciated in

64

that immortal document that made him the trusted champion of the movement to save the Union and free the slaves.

How could a man with Lincoln's lack of advantage to start with, with his lack of formal education, and with his lack of "opportunity"—how could he rise to the wonderful eminence which he obtained? It is a long reach from the humble cabin of an illiterate backwoodsman in Kentucky to the White House. It is a long reach from the boy that lay upon the puncheon floor in a frontier cabin, grasping in his hands the book he studied by the flickering light of a pine knot, to the man who could grasp a pen with which to write the Gettysburg Address and the Second Inaugural. If ever Browning's dictum that "a man's reach should exceed his grasp," was applicable to anybody, it was to Abraham Lincoln. He had an exceeding reach. He had "no form nor comeliness," and in him there was "no beauty that we should desire him"; but he had a beautiful soul. He was lean and lank and tall, but his tall body was not knee-high to his mind. His hands and feet were ungainly and big, but Lilliputian by comparison with his heart. His eyes were deep-set and dark circled with brooding upon the sorrows of his beloved country.

His father did not amount to much in himself, but he was the father of Abraham Lincoln, and that was sufficient glory for any one man. His mother died when he was a lad of nine, and the heartbroken boy took lonesome journeys to the lonely grave in the forest, and lured on by memories of her example and teachings, he journeyed to the far land of a noble life.

As a boy he had only a half-dozen books to read: *Robinson Crusoe, The Life of Washington,* the *History of the United States, Aesop's Fables,* the *Bible,* and *The Pilgrim's Progress.* But in his manhood, when the old Ship of State creaked and groaned in the stressful storm of war, his very strength made him as little understood by his fellows as was Robinson Crusoe by his man Friday on his far-off isle. His life in its noble traits outshone Weems's *Life of Washington* which he had studied. He became at once the type and flower of the Democracy of the United States whose history he had read, and he made more history than any other man of his day. He rivaled Aesop in the fables he told, setting all the world laughing at his homely yarns, even when a tempest of pain raged in his own heart. He translated the Bible into a version the common people understood easily—he translated it into life and character. His whole career was a *Pilgrim's Progress:* he floundered through many a Slough of Despond, he clambered up the steep Hill Difficulty, he faced lions in the way, he fought his way through the Valley of Humiliation and the Valley of the Shadow of Death, but he also reached the Delectable Mountains of service well done and the Beulah Land of Immortal Renown, and when he came to the River of Death, Mr. Good Conscience was there to ferry him over.

As a youth he helped the backwoodsmen at the "raisings" when they reared the rude log cabins where the settlers lived; as a man he held secure the ridge-pole of the house of State when a nation drunk with hate and internal strife threatened its destruction. In his youth he did not hesitate to besmirch his clothes by lifting a pig out of the mire where it was stuck; as a man he lifted up a race that wallowed in the mire of slavery and builded for it the temple of freedom. As a youth he trounced the rowdies of the backwoods who would steal from the store he kept; as a man he subdued the rowdies of the nation who fain would steal a single star from the flag of the Union he loved. As a child he learned his mother's will, and did it in such a way as to earn her encomiums; as a man he learned the direction in which God was going, and then, with all his splendid strength, moved things out of the way for Him!

LINCOLN'S SECOND INAUGURAL ADDRESS

The two greatest literary works that came out of the period of the Civil War were Lincoln's Gettysburg Address and his Second Inaugural. And of these, the Second Inaugural is the greater. It is brief. In its first sentence, he recognized that there was no occasion "for an extended address." Four years of terrible war, and the then recent course of events in that War tell their own story.

The Second Inaugural was delivered on the East Portico of the Capitol at noon on March 4, 1865. It had been raining early in the morning, and the whole forenoon was dark and cloudy. As Mr. Lincoln, with his tall, gaunt form, stepped out upon the East Portico, he lifted his hand to silence the cheering throng. For a moment he waited, as though memories were stirring his emotions, and then in a firm, clear voice, somewhat shrill and with an inexpressible pathos in it, he began his address. Just as he did so, through a rift in the clouds the sun shone full upon him. The clouds parted further until the whole sky was clear. The crowd regarded it as a good omen, and Lincoln confessed to the same feeling.

Finishing his Address, there was a moment of utter silence, and then applause; but the reception accorded his Address was as much marked by tears as by cheers, and, if the report of those present is to be accepted, even the applause had a note of solemnity in it.

The Address was variously received. No appraisement of it to us can be quite as interesting as that which Lincoln himself made. About ten days after the inauguration, Lincoln wrote a letter to his friend, Weed, in which he said:

Dear Mr. Weed:

Every one likes a compliment. Thank you for yours on my little notification speech and on the recent inaugural address. I expect the latter to wear as well as, perhaps better than, anything I have produced; but I believe it is not immediately popular.

Men are not flattered by being shown that there has been a difference of purpose between the Almighty and them. To deny it, however, in this case, is to deny that there is a God governing the world. It is a truth which I thought needed to be told, and, as whatever of humiliation there is in it falls most directly on myself, I thought others might afford for me to tell it.

Gladstone declared that he had been "taken captive" by the Address. "I see in it," he said, "the effect of sharp trial, when rightly borne, to raise men to higher level of thought and action. . . . Lincoln's words show that upon him anxiety and sorrow have wrought their true effect." The Second Inaugural contains the words of a man whose heart was deeply stirred, who, without conscious thought of art or effect, rose to heights of artless art. In his speech is something of the wild capricious poetry of life. His words are unsurpassed for simple beauty, dignity, and grandeur. They are lofty, manly, and Christian in sentiment. Lincoln was always powerful when he knew he was right. His whole nature responded to the appeal of justice. In this instance he was so well convinced that he was battling for truth and right that he was irresistible. It was the great heart of the wise-brained leader who gave us this gospel of concentrated truth, characterized by crystal clarity, with a rhythm of emotion that makes it well-nigh blank verse poetry. The scriptural cadences are freighted with a moral intensity.

It is easy enough to read this Address today, and to approve it; but if you wish to wonder at it, think yourself back into 1865, when hate, and fear, and prejudice, and bigotry, and intolerance stalked through the land. But in spite of such conditions, Lincoln kept his head. He never made an appeal to prejudice or to intolerance, or unfairness of any kind. Ten years before, Lincoln wrote to his friend, Joshua F. Speed, concerning the Know-Nothing Party which was then waging a national campaign. The Know-Nothing Party made appeals to prejudice similar to the Ku-Klux-Klan of a few years ago. Lincoln might have availed himself of the support of the Know-Nothings; but his attitude was expressed in this letter to Speed:

How can anyone who abhors the oppression of negroes be in favor of degrading classes of white people? Our progress in degeneracy appears to me to be pretty rapid. As a nation, we began by declaring that "all men are created equal." We now practically read it, "all men are created equal except negroes." When the Know-Nothings get control, it will read, "all men are created equal except negroes and foreigners and Catholics." When it comes to this, I shall prefer emigrating to some country where they make no pretense of loving liberty—to Russia, for instance, where despotism can be taken pure, and without the base alloy of hypocrisy.

Again, at the Republican Convention of 1856, he made a notable speech, in which he said, among other things: "Let us appeal to the sense and patriotism of the people, not to their prejudices; let us spread the floods of enthusiasm here aroused all over these vast prairies so suggestive of freedom. There is both a power and a magic in popular opinion. To that let us now appeal."

In a speech at Cincinnati, answering the question as to what he would do to those who opposed him if he were elected, he said: "We mean to remember that you are as good as we: that there is no difference between us other than the difference of circumstances. We mean to recognize and bear in mind always that you have as good hearts in your bosom as other people, or as we claim to have, and treat you accordingly."

On the night of his election for the second term, he responded to a crowd of serenaders by saying: "If I know my heart, my gratitude is free from any taint of personal triumph. I do not impugn the motives of anyone opposed to me."

Thus, there was a life of consistent tolerance and charity and fair dealing back of those great utterances in the Second Inaugural. Lincoln seemed able to see the other man's point of view. When he advocated tolerance, he required it of himself more than demanding it for himself. Many persons who loudly prate about tolerance, simply mean that they want you to be tolerant of them. Lincoln gave the example of showing tolerance toward others.

His great faith in God shines out all through the Second Inaugural: "The Almighty has His own purposes," he declared. Affirming and reaffirming his faith in the justice of his cause and in the righteousness of God, he comes to the last sentence of his brief Inaugural, a sentence that is one of the world's great utterances:

With malice toward none, with charity for all, with firmness in the right as God gives us to see the right, let us strive on to finish the work we are in, to bind up the nation's wounds, to care for him who shall have borne the battle and for his widow and his orphans, to do all which may achieve and cherish a just and a lasting peace among ourselves and with all nations.

The last clause of that gospel is a worthy text for every statesman today: "To do all which may achieve and cherish a just and a lasting peace among ourselves and with all nations."

CHAPTER VII

WOODROW WILSON'S "THE ROAD AWAY FROM REVOLUTION"

MANY epistles have been written on Americanism, but the one which I believe posterity a hundred or two hundred years from now will place along with the other writings included in this AMERICAN CANON is the last article that Woodrow Wilson ever wrote. It will be given this place partly because of the man who wrote it, and partly because of what it says.

With the possible exception of Thomas Jefferson, Woodrow Wilson was the keenest analytical mind that has ever occupied the White House. With the possible exceptions of George Washington and Abraham Lincoln, he stands without a peer as a patriot among all our Presidents. He was reviled and persecuted, vilified and lied about, but no more than were Washington and Lincoln in their days. For excellence of literary style, incisiveness of thought, and clarity of expression he stands unsurpassed.

Woodrow Wilson was a child of the parsonage, and throughout all his life the moral purposes and the Christian ideals of his Presbyterian preacher father held sway over him. His preparation for world leadership in an hour of crisis was perfect. Born in Virginia, brought up in the deeper South, and educated in the North, he had a sympathetic understanding of national history, which, added to his keen analytical powers, made him one of the most discriminating historians American scholarship has produced. As college professor, as university president, as governor of New Jersey, as President of the United States, he increased in mental stature and retained his moral ideals.

As President he showed his strength of leadership in keeping America out of war as long as he did, and then when America finally had to go into it, his intellectual powers and spiritual insight served the whole world well; for it was Woodrow Wilson who, after the War had been wallowing its bloody way across Europe for two years, seized it and lifted the whole ugly business up out of the sordid and the commercial and the revengeful, and put it on the high plane of moral purpose, and furnished ideals for the United States in entering it.

Although those ideals were lost in the long-continued and paralyzing discouragements and defeats that followed the War; although Wilson's own countrymen turned away from him when the applause had subsided, when all of the conditions were full of disillusion, and when depression and monotony made it easy to stop, yet Wilson stood fast to the doctrines of peace and justice and the settlement of international disputes by conference and understanding on the basis of good will which he had proclaimed when the whole world was acclaiming him its greatest leader.

Following his break in health and his retirement from the White House, Wilson was not able to carry on his more vigorous activities. Nevertheless, he kept mentally alert to what was happening. Mrs. Wilson tells us that in the spring of 1923 Woodrow Wilson began to display a sense of anxiety over the turn of affairs in the nation. He seemed to have a premonition of the troubles that finally did come in 1929 and following. He expressed a wish to write an article, but he had the use of only his right hand, and the return of neuritis in that hand made it practically impossible for him to hold a pen. He then turned to his typewriter again, but since he could pick out the letters with only one hand, he found that labor a burden. So he began to dictate to Mrs. Wilson what he wanted to say. Slowly, sometimes giving a single sentence in the middle of night, sometimes stopping in the midst of recreation and dictating another sentence, he finally had a short article written that he called *The Road Away From Revolution.* He polished the article again and again, smoothing up its diction, sharpening its style, making sure it said what he wanted it to say, and then he sent it to *The Atlantic Monthly,* in which it was published.

The article is as much of a warning against trends of selfishness and materialism in the nation as were the Epistles of Paul against certain evils that were manifesting themselves in the church in Corinth. He speaks of the universal unrest, and instead of hysterically denouncing everybody who talks about it, he pleads for a removal of the causes of social unrest. He thinks that these causes lie deeper than "mere economic blunders" or "superficial politics." He impeaches the "whole social system." He asks whether capitalists generally have "used their power for the benefit of the countries in which their capital is employed and for the benefit of their fellow men." He preaches the gospel of service and unselfishness in a way that would prompt certain "red baiters" of today to dub as "Communist" anybody else who would say the same things, but whose patriotism and Americanism were not so well established as Woodrow Wilson's. He was an American of the Americans. He was a patriot whose patriotism was tested as by fire. It would be well for us to listen to what he has to say, as he pleads for "a Christian conception of justice," and as he condemns "the too great selfishness of the capitalistic system." And then he concludes in these memorable words:

The sum of the whole matter is this, that our civilization cannot survive materially unless it be redeemed spiritually. It can be saved only by becoming permeated with the spirit of Christ and being made free and happy by the practices which spring out of that spirit. Only thus can discontent be driven out and all the shadows lifted from the road ahead.

Here is the final challenge to our churches, to our political organizations, and to our capitalists—to everyone who fears God or loves his country. Shall we not all earnestly co-operate to bring in the new day?

Wilson issues his challenge to our churches, to our political organizations, and to our capitalists, summoning them to co-operate in ushering in the new day. May it not easily be that the stress and strain of the bewildering world conditions confronting us are but the birth throes of a new era? Whether this new era is a potency for good or evil depends upon whether it is used selfishly or unselfishly; that is to say, whether it is Christian or materialistic. The spiritual conception of life is the only thing that can save society from a recrudescence of the jungle. Belief is important. A wrong head invariably eventuates in a wrong heart. A materialistic conception of life breeds low aims, selfishness, revenge.

President Wilson speaks of the capitalistic system. He accepts it as our logical system. It is certainly "logical" in the sense that it has had a natural growth. He would have this old system continue in the new day; but he also would warn us that the old spirit of greed and revenge and overreaching and selfishness is doomed as sure as there is a God.

Wilson says that discontent can be driven out and shadows lifted from the road ahead only by permeating civilization with the "spirit of Christ" and "by the practices which spring out of that spirit." Christ's standard of greatness was "whosoever would be great among you, let him be your servant." To compete for first place after the manner of Jesus means to serve, for the only greatness is service. When this rule obtains, men will point with pride to their industries and their business enterprises not because they pay big dividends, but because they contribute to human welfare. When Woodrow Wilson's bequest of the "spirit of Christ" is accepted and made operative by mankind, men will not strive early and late to get gain for themselves, but to help others to find a richer, fuller life.

IN conclusion, it is appropriate to give a summary of the most sovereign ideas and ideals of THE AMERICAN CANON. Let us recall the sapient dictum of James Russell Lowell that our American republic will endure "as long as the ideas of the men who founded it continue dominant." These ideas are expressed in the seven writings which we have now studied, writings that differ as much from one another as the various books of the Bible differ one from another. The varying books of the Bible were finally included in the sacred volume because they measured up to certain standards, particularly because they were repositories of religious truth, and revealed God to man, and man's dependence upon God, and the working out of God's divine will among the children of men. So, these seven American writings differ one from another, but they are bound together by the golden thread of the American spirit, the genius of America. One divine drive of purposive idealism breathes through all of them. Taken as a whole, we discover from them what America is, and we find in them the definition of Americanism.

It is important that the ideas and the ideals of the founding fathers of our republic should be rehearsed to each new generation—and especially to the present generation, for the world is confronted today with two irreconcilably divergent theories of government. On the one hand is the totalitarian state. In it the powers and responsibilities of government

75

are precisely focused in one person, the Dictator. He has waded to his seat of authority through crimson seas of carnage. He holds his power by physical force and violence. Liberty of opinion does not exist. The firing squad and the concentration camp have put the quietus upon freedom of speech and freedom of the press. The pulpit is subservient to the whims of the Dictator—being required to render unto Caesar the things that are God's. Education is trammeled to serve the ends of the totalitarian state, fawning before the flattery of the Dictator, or cringing before his denunciation. Bigotry and intolerance, proscription and persecution are all invoked in the name of the country's good, and are accepted under the illusion of efficiency.

On the other hand is Democracy. It may not be as efficient at a given moment as a dictatorship; but the only way to develop a people is to shoulder them with the responsibility of directing their own affairs, of shaping their own objectives and of determining their own progress. The alleged efficiency of a dictatorship is bought at a frightful cost—a cost that no sane people will ever voluntarily pay. Democracy rests upon the theory that governments derive their just powers from the consent of the governed. It holds that government is made for man, not man for the government. It assumes that the people need institutions, and that in time of institutional crisis the people can be trusted to save, or modify, or remake their institutions. It protects liberty of opinion, and freedom of speech and of the press as its very breath of life. It guarantees the free exercise of religion, knowing that religion inheres in the nature of man, and is vital and intelligent only when it is called forth by the experiences of life. It safeguards the freedom of the pulpit, learning therefrom its moral sense of direction. It defends the academic freedom of the schools, recognizing that democracy's real problem is to develop an

76

intelligence equal to its social responsibility: otherwise men are likely to regard democratic institutions as ends in themselves, keeping them static instead of dynamic, and holding the parchments of historic documents as worth more than the gains they record.

Through *The American Canon* breathes the spirit of tolerance. These great writings give no place to musty prejudices, whether racial, religious, social, or otherwise. Democracy is an attitude of mind, a condition of soul. It is therefore worse than hypocritical for a professed believer in democracy to become an intolerant persecutor of persons who happen not to accept his own political creed. The intelligent and historically true American patriot knows that the cure for the ills of democracy is more democracy. It is ridiculous to credit a man with being democratic merely because he becomes intolerant in his defense of some document of democracy.

Democracy was a dominant idea of the men who founded our republic. The trouble with us is that when we think of democracy, we think of certain mechanisms of government. In reality, democracy is a spirit. Democracy finds its sanction in the nature of man. Man was meant to be free. Democracy is a state of society in which government is dedicated to the service of human need and has for its supreme aim the furtherance of human progress. In our American democratic system, we conceive of government as the servant of the people, subject always to the enlightened will of the people. With us, power is responsibility.

Equality of opportunity and equality before the law are essential American doctrines. Carved in the marble over the entrance to the magnificent new home of the Supreme Court of the United States, in Washington, D. C., are the words: "Equal justice under law." That doctrine will be given hands and feet by every true American.

The authors of the Mayflower Compact declared that they would enact just and equal laws, and then solemnly pledged themselves to give due and reverent obedience to those laws. Likewise, reverence for law stands out on every page of *The American Canon*. Abraham Lincoln speaks for all true Americans when he says:

Let every American, every lover of liberty, every well-wisher of his posterity, swear by the blood of the Revolution never to violate in the least particular the laws of the country, and never to tolerate their violation by others. As the patriots of Seventy-six did to the support of the Declaration of Independence, so to the support of the Constitution and laws let every American pledge his life, his property, and his sacred honor. Let every man remember that to violate the law is to trample on the blood of his fathers and to tear the charter of his own and his children's liberty. Let reverence for the laws be breathed by every American mother to the lisping babe that prattles on her lap; let it be taught in schools, in seminaries, and in colleges; let it be written in primers, spelling books and almanacs; let it be preached from pulpit, proclaimed in the legislative halls, and enforced in courts of justice. In short, let it become the political religion of the nation.

Obedience is not always synonymous with subordination. There can be no true liberty without limitations, no true freedom without recognition of restricting responsibilities, no true democracy without personal self-control. Socrates called morality the art of self-possession and self-government. The one fundamental virtue, he taught, was "rule over oneself."

We have seen again and again in our study of *The American Canon* that a regnant idea of the men who fashioned our republic was freedom to worship God. The reverse side of this idea is their own personal faith in God. They worshiped God, and they wanted others to have the right to worship Him. Any right to be kept must be used. Our fathers worshiped God because they believed in Him. Their lives were God-centered. Their faith in God lent all their work an unspeakable solemnity and moral significance.

They believed in prayer, and expressed their belief in their words not only, but by praying to the Almighty.

They believed in the Bible. Our great American leaders from the beginning to the present, almost without exception, have been loyal to the Bible. What George Washington said would have been approved by almost all his compatriots, namely: "Above all, the pure and benign light of Revelation has had a meliorating influence on mankind, and increased the blessings of society." What Ulysses S. Grant declared would be subscribed to by nearly all of those who have shaped the American spirit: "Hold fast to the Bible as the sheet anchor of your liberties; write its precepts on your hearts and practice them in your lives. To the influence of this book we are indebted for the progress made in civilization, and to this we must look as our guide in the future." These expressions are given not because they are exceptional, but because they are typical of the belief of the greatest Americans.

Education is another need made apparent by a study of the foundations of American democracy. Many people get wrought up over what they call "subversive influences" and "subversive activities." The thing that the Fascist or the Communist is most afraid of is unregimented education. I wish our victims of Communist-phobia could understand that you cannot kill an idea by damning, or imprisoning, or shooting somebody who holds it. The way to get rid of an idea is to supplant it with a better one. The surest way to disseminate the right idea is by education. Acquaintance-ship of our American people with the great documents which

I have brought together in *The American Canon* will do more to overcome subversive activities and influences than all the red-baiting and railing at Communists indulged in during the past twenty-five years. And while filling the mind with the doctrine of true Americanism, the intelligent patriot will earnestly try to remove the causes of social discontent.

No people's rule over itself is safe unless there be intelligence, morality, and a great faith in God. When a people undertake to do their own dictatorship they assume the responsibilities as well as the privileges of the function. Therefore, education must be as widely diffused as the right of suffrage, for only an intelligent people is fit to govern itself. Education must develop a sense of values, for it is only when a people have a sense of moral direction that they are fit to take into their own hands the helm of the Ship of State.

APPENDIX

THE ROAD AWAY FROM REVOLUTION[1]

BY WOODROW WILSON

IN these doubtful and anxious days, when all the world is at
unrest, and, look which way you will, the road ahead seems dark-
ened by shadows which portend dangers of many kinds, it is only
common prudence that we should look about us and attempt to
assess the causes of distress and the most likely means of removing
them.

There must be some real ground for the universal unrest and
perturbation. It is not to be found in superficial politics or in
mere economic blunders. It probably lies deep at the sources
of the spiritual life of our time. It leads to revolution; and perhaps if we take the case of the Russian Revolution, the outstanding
event of its kind in our age, we may find a good deal of instruc-
tion for our judgment of present critical situations and circumstances.

What gave rise to the Russian Revolution? The answer can
only be that it was the product of a whole social system. It was
not, in fact, a sudden thing. It had been gathering head for
several generations. It was due to the systematic denial to the
great body of Russians of the rights and privileges which all
normal men desire and must have if they are to be contented
and within reach of happiness. The lives of the great mass of the
Russian people contained no opportunities, but were hemmed
in by barriers against which they were constantly flinging their
spirits, only to fall back bruised and dispirited. Only the powerful were suffered to secure their rights or even to gain access to
the means of material success.

It is to be noted as a leading fact of our time that it was against
"capitalism" that the Russian leaders directed their attack. It
was capitalism that made them see red; and it is against capitalism
under one name or another that the discontented classes every-
where draw their indictment.

There are thoughtful and well-informed men all over the world

81

who believe, with much apparently sound reason, that the abstract thing, the system, which we call capitalism, is indispensable to the industrial support and development of modern civilization. And yet everyone who has an intelligent knowledge of social forces must know that great and widespread reactions like that which is now unquestionably manifesting itself against capitalism do not occur without cause or provocation; and before we commit ourselves irreconcilably to an attitude of hostility to this movement of the time, we ought frankly to put to ourselves the question, Is the capitalistic system unimpeachable? which is another way of asking, Have capitalists generally used their power for the benefit of the countries in which their capital is employed and for the benefit of their fellow men?

Is it not, on the contrary, too true that capitalists have often seemed to regard the men whom they used as mere instruments of profit, whose physical and mental powers it was legitimate to exploit with as slight cost to themselves as possible, either of money or of sympathy? Have not many fine men who were actuated by the highest principles in every other relationship of life seemed to hold that generosity and humane feeling were not among the imperative mandates of conscience in the conduct of a banking business, or in the development of an industrial or commercial enterprise?

And, if these offenses against high morality and true citizenship have been frequently observable, are we to say that the blame for the present discontent and turbulence is wholly on the side of those who are in revolt against them? Ought we not, rather, to seek a way to remove such offenses and make life itself clean for those who will share honorably and cleanly in it?

The world has been made safe for democracy. There need now be no fear that any such mad design as that entertained by the insolent and ignorant Hohenzollerns and their counselors may prevail against it. But democracy has not yet made the world safe against irrational revolution. That supreme task, which is nothing less than the salvation of civilization, now faces democracy, insistent, imperative. There is no escaping it, unless everything we have built up is presently to fall in ruin about us; and the United States, as the greatest of democracies, must undertake it.

The road that leads away from revolution is clearly marked, for it is defined by the nature of men and of organized society. It therefore behooves us to study very carefully and very candidly the exact nature of the task and the means of its accomplishment.

APPENDIX

The nature of men and of organized society dictates the maintenance in every field of action of the highest and purest standards of justice and of right dealing; and it is essential to efficacious thinking in this critical matter that we should not entertain a narrow or technical conception of justice. By justice the lawyer generally means the prompt, fair, and open application of impartial rules; but we call ours a Christian civilization, and a Christian conception of justice must be much higher. It must include sympathy and helpfulness and a willingness to forgo self-interest in order to promote the welfare, happiness, and contentment of others and of the community as a whole. This is what our age is blindly feeling after in its reaction against what it deems the too great selfishness of the capitalistic system.

The sum of the whole matter is this, that our civilization cannot survive materially unless it be redeemed spiritually. It can be saved only by becoming permeated with the spirit of Christ and being made free and happy by the practices which spring out of that spirit. Only thus can discontent be driven out and all the shadows lifted from the road ahead.

Here is the final challenge to our churches, to our political organizations, and to our capitalists—to everyone who fears God or loves his country. Shall we not all earnestly co-operate to bring in the new day?

THE STAR-SPANGLED BANNER

Francis Scott Key
(1780–1843)

John Stafford Smith
(1750–1836)

1. Oh,— say, can you see by the dawn's ear-ly light What so
2. On the shore, dim-ly seen thro' the mists of the deep, Where the
3. Oh,— thus be it ev-er when— free-men shall stand Be-

proud-ly we hail'd at the twi-light's last gleam-ing, Whose broad
foe's haught-y host in dread si-lence re-pos-es, What is
tween their loved homes and the war's des-o-la-tion! Blest with

stripes and bright stars, thro' the per-il-ous fight, O'er the ram-parts we
that which the breeze, o'er the tow-er-ing steep, As it fit-ful-ly
vic-t'ry and peace, may the heav'n-res-cued land Praise the Pow'r that hath

watch'd were so gal-lant-ly stream-ing? And the rock-ets' red
blows, half con-ceals, half dis-clos-es? Now it catch-es the
made and pre-serv'd us a na-tion! Then— con-quer we

glare, the bombs burst-ing in air, Gave proof thro' the night that our
gleam of the morn-ing's first beam, In full glo-ry re-flect-ed now—
must, when our cause it is just, And— this be our mot-to: "In——
broader

flag was still there. Oh, say, does that Star-span-gled Ban-ner— yet—
shines on the stream. 'Tis the Star-span-gled Ban-ner, oh, long may— it—
God is our Trust." And the Star-span-gled Ban-ner in tri-umph shall
very broad *rall.*

wave— O'er the land— of the free and the home of the brave?
wave— O'er the land— of the free and the home of the brave!
wave— O'er the land— of the free and the home of the brave.

LINCOLN'S SECOND INAUGURAL ADDRESS
MARCH 4, 1865

FELLOW-COUNTRYMEN: At this second appearing to take the oath of the Presidential office, there is less occasion for an extended address than there was at the first. Then a statement somewhat in detail of a course to be pursued seemed very fitting and proper. Now, at the expiration of four years, during which public declarations have been constantly called forth on every point and phase of the great contest which still absorbs the attention and engrosses the energies of the nation, little that is new could be presented.

The progress of our arms, upon which all else chiefly depends, is as well known to the public as to myself; and it is, I trust, reasonably satisfactory and encouraging to all. With high hope for the future, no prediction in regard to it is ventured.

On the occasion corresponding to this, four years ago, all thoughts were anxiously directed to an impending civil war. All dreaded it; all sought to avoid it. While the inaugural address was being delivered from this place, devoted altogether to saving the Union without war, insurgent agents were in the city seeking to destroy it without war—seeking to dissolve the Union and divide the effects by negotiation. Both parties deprecated war; but one of them would make war rather than let the nation survive, and the other would accept war rather than let it perish; and the war came.

One eighth of the whole population were colored slaves, not distributed generally over the Union, but localized in the southern part of it. These slaves constituted a peculiar and powerful interest. All knew that this interest was somehow the cause of the war. To strengthen, perpetuate, and extend this interest, was the object for which the insurgents would rend the Union even by war, while the government claimed no right to do more than to restrict the territorial enlargement of it.

Neither party expected for the war the magnitude or the duration which it has already attained. Neither anticipated that the cause of the conflict might cease with, or even before, the conflict itself should cease. Each looked for an easier triumph, and a result less fundamental and astounding.

Both read the same Bible and pray to the same God, and each

invokes his aid against the other. It may seem strange that any men should dare to ask a just God's assistance in wringing their bread from the sweat of other men's faces; but let us judge not, that we be not judged. The prayers of both could not be answered. That of neither has been answered fully. The Almighty has his own purposes. "Woe unto the world because of offenses, for it must needs be that offenses come; but woe to that man by whom the offense cometh." If we shall suppose that American slavery is one of these offenses, which in the providence of God must needs come, but which, having continued through his appointed time, he now wills to remove, and that he gives to both North and South this terrible war as the woe due to those by whom the offense came, shall we discern therein any departure from those divine attributes which the believers in a living God always ascribe to him? Fondly do we hope, fervently do we pray, that this mighty scourge of war may soon pass away. Yet, if God wills that it continue until all the wealth piled by the bondman's two hundred and fifty years of unrequited toil shall be sunk, and until every drop of blood drawn with the lash shall be paid with another drawn with the sword; as was said three thousand years ago, so still it must be said, "The judgments of the Lord are true and righteous altogether."

With malice toward none, with charity for all, with firmness in the right as God gives us to see the right, let us strive on to finish the work we are in, to bind up the nation's wounds, to care for him who shall have borne the battle and for his widow and orphans, to do all which may achieve and cherish a just and a lasting peace among ourselves and with all nations.

WASHINGTON'S FAREWELL ADDRESS
TO THE PEOPLE OF THE UNITED STATES

FRIENDS AND FELLOW-CITIZENS:

The period for a new election of a citizen, to administer the executive government of the United States, being not far distant, and the time actually arrived, when your thoughts must be employed in designating the person, who is to be clothed with that important trust, it appears to me proper, especially as it may conduce to a more distinct expression of the public voice, that I should now apprize you of the resolution I have formed, to decline being considered among the number of those, out of whom a choice is to be made.

I beg you, at the same time, to do me the justice to be assured, that this resolution has not been taken without a strict regard to all the considerations appertaining to the relation, which binds a dutiful citizen to his country; and that, in withdrawing the tender of service, which silence in my situation might imply, I am influenced by no diminution of zeal for your future interest; no deficiency of grateful respect for your past kindness; but am supported by a full conviction that the step is compatible with both.

The acceptance of, and continuance hitherto in, the office to which your suffrages have twice called me, have been a uniform sacrifice of inclination to the opinion of duty, and to a deference for what appeared to be your desire. I constantly hoped, that it would have been much earlier in my power, consistently with motives, which I was not at liberty to disregard, to return to that retirement, from which I had been reluctantly drawn. The strength of my inclination to do this, previous to the last election, had even led to the preparation of an address to declare it to you; but mature reflection on the then perplexed and critical posture of our affairs with foreign nations, and the unanimous advice of persons entitled to my confidence, impelled me to abandon the idea.

I rejoice, that the state of your concerns, external as well as internal, no longer renders the pursuit of inclination incompatible with the sentiment of duty, or propriety; and am persuaded, whatever partiality may be retained for my services, that, in the present circumstances of our country, you will not disapprove my determination to retire.

The impressions, with which I first undertook the arduous trust, were explained on the proper occasion. In the discharge of this trust, I will only say, that I have, with good intentions, contributed towards the organization and administration of the government the best exertions of which a very fallible judgment was capable. Not unconscious, in the outset, of the inferiority of my qualifications, experience in my own eyes, perhaps still more in the eyes of others, has strengthened the motives to diffidence of myself; and every day the increasing weight of years admonishes me more and more, that the shade of retirement is as necessary to me as it will be welcome. Satisfied, that, if any circumstances have given peculiar value to my services, they were temporary, I have the consolation to believe, that, while choice and prudence invite me to quit the political scene, patriotism does not forbid it.

In looking forward to the moment, which is intended to terminate the career of my public life, my feelings do not permit me to suspend the deep acknowledgment of that debt of gratitude, which I owe to my beloved country for the many honors it has conferred upon me; still more for the steadfast confidence with which it has supported me; and for the opportunities I have thence enjoyed of manifesting my inviolable attachment, by services faithful and persevering, though in usefulness unequal to my zeal. If benefits have resulted to our country from these services, let it always be remembered to your praise, and as an instructive example in our annals, that under circumstances in which the passions, agitated in every direction, were liable to mislead, amidst appearances sometimes dubious, vicissitudes of fortune often discouraging, in situations in which not unfrequently want of success has countenanced the spirit of criticism, the constancy of your support was the essential prop of the efforts, and a guarantee of the plans by which they were effected. Profoundly penetrated with this idea, I shall carry it with me to my grave, as a strong incitement to unceasing vows that Heaven may continue to you the choicest tokens of its beneficence; that your union and brotherly affection may be perpetual; that the free constitution, which is the work of your hands, may be sacredly maintained; that its administration in every department may be stamped with wisdom and virtue; that, in fine, the happiness of the people of these States, under the auspices of liberty, may be made complete, by so careful a preservation and so prudent a use of this blessing, as will acquire to them the glory of recommending it to the applause, the affection, and adoption of every nation, which is yet a stranger to it.

Here, perhaps, I ought to stop. But a solicitude for your welfare, which cannot end but with my life, and the apprehension of danger, natural to that solicitude, urge me, on an occasion like the present, to offer to your solemn contemplation, and to recommend to your frequent review, some sentiments, which are the result of much reflection, of no inconsiderable observation, and which appear to me all-important to the permanency of your felicity as a People. These will be offered to you with the more freedom, as you can only see in them the disinterested warnings of a parting friend, who can possibly have no personal motive to bias his counsel. Nor can I forget, as an encouragement to it, your indulgent reception of my sentiments on a former and not dissimilar occasion.

Interwoven as is the love of liberty with every ligament of your hearts, no recommendation of mine is necessary to fortify or confirm the attachment.

The unity of Government, which constitutes you one people, is also now dear to you. It is justly so: for it is a main pillar in the edifice of your real independence, the support of your tranquillity at home, your peace abroad; of your safety; of your prosperity; of that very Liberty, which you so highly prize. But as it is easy to foresee, that, from different causes and from different quarters, much pains will be taken, many artifices employed, to weaken in your minds the conviction of this truth; as this is the point in your political fortress against which the batteries of internal and external enemies will be most constantly and actively (though often covertly and insidiously) directed, it is of infinite moment, that you should properly estimate the immense value of your national Union to your collective and individual happiness; that you should cherish a cordial, habitual, and immovable attachment to it; accustoming yourselves to think and speak of it as of the Palladium of your political safety and prosperity; watching for its preservation with jealous anxiety; discountenancing whatever may suggest even a suspicion, that it can in any event be abandoned; and indignantly frowning upon the first dawning of every attempt to alienate any portion of our country from the rest, or to enfeeble the sacred ties which now link together the various parts.

For this you have every inducement of sympathy and interest. Citizens, by birth or choice, of a common country, that country has a right to concentrate your affections. The name of AMERICAN, which belongs to you, in your national capacity, must always exalt the just pride of Patriotism, more than any appellation derived from local discriminations. With slight shades of difference, you have the same religion, manners,· habits, and political principles. You have in a common cause fought and triumphed together; the Independence and Liberty you possess are the work of joint counsels, and joint efforts, of common dangers, sufferings, and successes.

But these considerations, however powerfully they address themselves to your sensibility, are greatly outweighed by those which apply more immediately to your interest. Here every portion of our country finds the most commanding motives for carefully guarding and preserving the Union of the whole.

The *North*, in an unrestrained intercouse with the *South*, protected by the equal laws of a common government, finds, in the productions of the latter, great additional resources of maritime and commercial enterprise and precious materials of manufacturing industry. The *South*, in the same intercourse, benefiting by the agency of the *North*, sees its agriculture grow and its commerce expand. Turning partly into its own channels the seamen of the *North*, it finds its particular navigation invigorated; and, while it contributes, in different ways, to nourish and increase the general mass of the national navigation, it looks forward to the protection of a maritime strength, to which itself is unequally adapted. The *East*, in a like intercourse with the *West*, already finds, and in the progressive improvement of interior communications by land and water, will more and more find, a valuable vent for the commodities which it brings from abroad, or manufactures at home. The *West* derives from the *East* supplies requisite to its growth and comfort, and, what is perhaps of still greater consequence, it must of necessity owe the *secure* enjoyment of indispensable *outlets* for its own productions to the weight, influence, and the future maritime strength of the Atlantic side of the Union, directed by an indissoluble community of interest as *one nation*. Any other tenure by which the *West* can hold this essential advantage, whether derived from its own separate strength, or from an apostate and unnatural connexion with any foreign power, must be intrinsically precarious.

While, then, every part of our country thus feels an immediate and particular interest in Union, all the parts combined cannot fail to find in the united mass of means and efforts greater strength, greater resource, proportionably greater security from external danger, a less frequent interruption of their peace by foreign nations; and, what is of inestimable value, they must derive from Union an exemption from those broils and wars between themselves, which so frequently afflict neighbouring countries not tied together by the same governments, which their own rivalships alone would be sufficient to produce, but which opposite foreign alliances, attachments, and intrigues would stimulate and embitter. Hence, likewise, they will avoid the necessity of those overgrown military establishments, which, under any form of government, are inauspicious to liberty, and which are to be regarded as particularly hostile to Republican Liberty. In this sense it is, that your Union ought to be considered as a main prop of your liberty, and that the love of the one ought to endear to you the preservation of the other.

These considerations speak a persuasive language to every reflecting and virtuous mind, and exhibit the continuance of the UNION as a primary object of Patriotic desire. Is there a doubt, whether a common government can embrace so large a sphere? Let experience solve it. To listen to mere speculation in such a case were criminal. We are authorized to hope, that a proper organization of the whole, with the auxiliary agency of governments for the respective subdivisions, will afford a happy issue to the experiment. It is well worth a fair and full experiment. With such powerful and obvious motives to Union, affecting all parts of our country, while experience shall not have demonstrated its impracticability, there will always be reason to distrust the patriotism of those, who in any quarter may endeavour to weaken its bands.

In contemplating the causes, which may disturb our Union, it occurs as matter of serious concern, that any ground should have been furnished for characterizing parties by *Geographical* discriminations, *Northern* and *Southern*, *Atlantic* and *Western;* whence designing men may endeavour to excite a belief, that there is a real difference of local interests and views. One of the expedients of party to acquire influence, within particular districts, is to misrepresent the opinions and aims of other districts. You cannot shield yourselves too much against the jealousies and heart-burnings, which spring from these misrepresentations; they tend to render alien to each other those, who ought to be bound together by fraternal affection. The inhabitants of our western country have lately had a useful lesson on this head; they have seen, in the negotiation by the Executive, and in the unanimous ratification by the Senate, of the treaty with Spain, and in the universal satisfaction at that event, throughout the United States, a decisive proof how unfounded were the suspicions propagated among them of a policy in the General Government and in the Atlantic States unfriendly to their interests in regard to the MISSISSIPPI; they have been witnesses to the formation of two treaties, that with Great Britain, and that with Spain, which secure to them every thing they could desire, in respect to our foreign relations, towards confirming their prosperity. Will it not be their wisdom to rely for the preservation of these advantages on the UNION by which they were procured? Will they not henceforth be deaf to those advisers, if such there are, who would sever them from their brethren, and connect them with aliens?

To the efficacy and permanency of your Union, a Government for the whole is indispensable. No alliances, however strict, between the parts can be an adequate substitute; they must inevitably experience the infractions and interruptions, which all alliances in all times have experienced. Sensible of this momentous truth, you have improved upon your first essay, by the adoption of a Constitution of Government better calculated than your former for an intimate Union, and for the efficacious management of your common concerns. This Government, the offspring of our own choice, uninfluenced and unawed, adopted upon full investigation and mature deliberation, completely free in its principles, in the distribution of its powers, uniting security with energy, and containing within itself a provision for its own amendment, has a just claim to your confidence and your support. Respect for its authority, compliance with its laws, acquiescence in its measures, are duties enjoined by the fundamental maxims of true Liberty. The basis of our political systems is the right of the people to make and to alter their Constitutions of Government. But the Constitution which at any time exists, till changed by an explicit and authentic act of the whole people, is sacredly obligatory upon all. The very idea of the power and the right of the people to establish Government presupposes the duty of every individual to obey the established Government.

APPENDIX

All obstructions to the execution of the Laws, all combinations and associations, under whatever plausible character, with the real design to direct, control, counteract, or awe the regular deliberation and action of the constituted authorities, are destructive of this fundamental principle, and of fatal tendency. They serve to organize faction, to give it an artificial and extraordinary force; to put, in the place of the delegated will of the nation, the will of a party, often a small but artful and enterprising minority of the community; and, according to the alternate triumphs of different parties, to make the public administration the mirror of the ill-concerted and incongruous projects of faction, rather than the organ of consistent and wholesome plans digested by common counsels, and modified by mutual interests.

However combinations or associations of the above descriptions may now and then answer popular ends, they are likely, in the course of time and things, to become potent engines, by which cunning, ambitious, and unprincipled men will be enabled to subvert the power of the people, and to usurp for themselves the reins of government; destroying afterwards the very engines, which have lifted them to unjust dominion.

Towards the preservation of your government, and the permanency of your present happy state, it is requisite, not only that you steadily discountenance irregular oppositions to its acknowledged authority, but also that you resist with care the spirit of innovation upon its principles, however specious the pretexts. One method of assault may be to effect, in the forms of the constitution, alterations, which will impair the energy of the system, and thus to undermine what cannot be directly overthrown. In all the changes to which you may be invited, remember that time and habit are at least as necessary to fix the true character of governments, as of other human institutions; that experience is the surest standard, by which to test the real tendency of the existing constitution of a country; that facility in changes, upon the credit of mere hypothesis and opinion, exposes to perpetual change, from the endless variety of hypothesis and opinion; and remember, especially, that, for the efficient management of your common interests, in a country so extensive as ours, a government of as much vigor as is consistent with the perfect security of liberty is indispensable. Liberty itself will find in such a government, with powers properly distributed and adjusted, its surest guardian. It is, indeed, little else than a

93

name, where the government is too feeble to withstand the enterprise of faction, to confine each member of the society within the limits prescribed by the laws, and to maintain all in the secure and tranquil enjoyment of the rights of person and property.

I have already intimated to you the danger of parties in the state, with particular reference to the founding of them on geographical discriminations. Let me now take a more comprehensive view, and warn you in the most solemn manner against the baneful effects of the spirit of party, generally.

This spirit, unfortunately, is inseparable from our nature, having its root in the strongest passions of the human mind. It exists under different shapes in all governments, more or less stifled, controlled, or repressed; but, in those of the popular form, it is seen in its greatest rankness, and is truly their worst enemy.

The alternate domination of one faction over another, sharpened by the spirit of revenge, natural to party dissension, which in different ages and countries has perpetrated the most horrid enormities, is itself a frightful despotism. But this leads at length to a more formal and permanent despotism. The disorders and miseries, which result, gradually incline the minds of men to seek security and repose in the absolute power of an individual; and sooner or later the chief of some prevailing faction, more able or more fortunate than his competitors, turns this disposition to the purposes of his own elevation, on the ruins of Public Liberty.

Without looking forward to an extremity of this kind, (which nevertheless ought not to be entirely out of sight,) the common and continual mischiefs of the spirit of party are sufficient to make it the interest and duty of a wise people to discourage and restrain it.

It serves always to distract the Public Councils, and enfeeble the Public Administration. It agitates the Community with ill-founded jealousies and false alarms; kindles the animosity of one part against another, foments occasionally riot and insurrection. It opens the door to foreign influence and corruption, which find a facilitated access to the government itself through the channels of party passions. Thus the policy and the will of one country are subjected to the policy and will of another.

There is an opinion, that parties in free countries are useful checks upon the administration of the Government, and serve to keep alive the spirit of Liberty. This within certain limits is probably true; and in Governments of a Monarchical cast, Patriotism may look with indulgence, if not with favor, upon the spirit of party. But in those of the popular character, in Governments purely elective, it is a spirit not to be encouraged. From their natural tendency, it is certain there will always be enough of that spirit for every salutary purpose. And, there being constant danger of excess, the effort ought to be, by force of public opinion, to mitigate and assuage it. A fire not to be quenched, it demands a uniform vigilance to prevent its bursting into a flame, lest, instead of warming, it should consume.

It is important, likewise, that the habits of thinking in a free country should inspire caution, in those intrusted with its administration, to confine themselves within their respective constitutional spheres, avoiding in the exercise of the powers of one department to encroach upon another. The spirit of encroachment tends to consolidate the powers of all the departments in one, and thus to create, whatever the form of government, a real despotism. A just estimate of that love of power, and proneness to abuse it, which predominates in the human heart, is sufficient to satisfy us of the truth of this position. The necessity of reciprocal checks in the exercise of political power, by dividing and distributing it into different depositories, and constituting each the Guardian of the Public Weal against invasions by the others, has been evinced by experiments ancient and modern; some of them in our country and under our own eyes. To preserve them must be as necessary as to institute them. If, in the opinion of the people, the distribution or modification of the constitutional powers be in any particular wrong, let it be corrected by an amendment in the way, which the constitution designates. But let there be no change by usurpation; for, though this, in one instance, may be the instrument of good, it is the customary weapon by which free governments are destroyed. The precedent must always greatly overbalance in permanent evil any partial or transient benefit, which the use can at any time yield.

Of all the dispositions and habits, which lead to political prosperity, Religion and Morality are indispensable supports. In vain would that man claim the tribute of Patriotism, who should labor to subvert these great pillars of human happiness, these firmest props of the duties of Men and Citizens. The mere Politician, equally with the pious man, ought to respect and to cherish them. A volume could not trace all their connexions with private and public felicity. Let it simply be asked,

Where is the security for property, for reputation, for life, if the sense of religious obligation *desert* the oaths, which are the instruments of investigation in Courts of Justice? And let us with caution indulge the supposition, that morality can be maintained without religion. Whatever may be conceded to the influence of refined education on minds of peculiar structure, reason and experience both forbid us to expect, that national morality can prevail in exclusion of religious principle.

It is substantially true, that virtue or morality is a necessary spring of popular government. The rule, indeed, extends with more or less force to every species of free government. Who, that is a sincere friend to it, can look with indifference upon attempts to shake the foundation of the fabric?

Promote, then, as an object of primary importance, institutions for the general diffusion of knowledge. In proportion as the structure of a government gives force to public opinion, it is essential that public opinion should be enlightened.

As a very important source of strength and security, cherish public credit. One method of preserving it is, to use it as sparingly as possible; avoiding occasions of expense by cultivating peace, but remembering also that timely disbursements to prepare for danger frequently prevent much greater disbursements to repel it; avoiding likewise the accumulation of debt, not only by shunning occasions of expense, but by vigorous exertions in time of peace to discharge the debts, which unavoidable wars may have occasioned, not ungenerously throwing upon posterity the burthen, which we ourselves ought to bear. The execution of these maxims belongs to your representatives, but it is necessary that public opinion should coöperate. To facilitate to them the performance of their duty, it is essential that you should practically bear in mind, that towards the payment of debts there must be Revenue; that to have Revenue there must be taxes; that no taxes can be devised, which are not more or less inconvenient and unpleasant, that the intrinsic embarrassment, inseparable from the selection of the proper objects (which is always a choice of difficulties), ought to be a decisive motive for a candid construction of the conduct of the government in making it, and for a spirit of acquiescence in the measures for obtaining revenue, which the public exigencies may at any time dictate.

Observe good faith and justice towards all Nations; cultivate peace and harmony with all. Religion and Morality enjoin this conduct; and can it be, that good policy does not equally enjoin it? It will be worthy of a free, enlightened, and, at no distant period, a great Nation, to give to mankind the magnanimous and too novel example of a people always guided by an exalted justice and benevolence. Who can doubt, that, in the course of time and things, the fruits of such a plan would richly repay any temporary advantages, which might be lost by a steady adherence to it? Can it be, that Providence has not connected the permanent felicity of a Nation with its Virtue? The experiment, at least, is recommended by every sentiment which ennobles human nature. Alas! is it rendered impossible by its vices?

In the execution of such a plan, nothing is more essential, than that permanent, inveterate antipathies against particular Nations, and passionate attachments for others, should be excluded; and that, in place of them, just and amicable feelings towards all should be cultivated. The Nation, which indulges towards another an habitual hatred, or an habitual fondness, is in some degree a slave. It is a slave to its animosity or to its affection, either of which is sufficient to lead it astray from its duty and its interest. Antipathy in one nation against another disposes each more readily to offer insult and injury, to lay hold of slight causes of umbrage, and to be haughty and intractable, when accidental or trifling occasions of dispute occur. Hence frequent collisions, obstinate, envenomed, and bloody contests. The Nation, prompted by ill-will and resentment, sometimes impels to war the Government, contrary to the best calculations of policy. The Government sometimes participates in the national propensity, and adopts through passion what reason would reject; at other times, it makes the animosity of the nation subservient to projects of hostility instigated by pride, ambition, and other sinister and pernicious motives. The peace often, sometimes perhaps the liberty, of Nations has been the victim.

So likewise, a passionate attachment of one Nation for another produces a variety of evils. Sympathy for the favorite Nation, facilitating the illusion of an imaginary common interest, in cases where no real common interest exists, and infusing into one the enmities of the other, betrays the former into a participation in the quarrels and wars of the latter, without adequate inducement or justification. It leads also to concessions to the favorite Nation of privileges denied to others, which is apt doubly to injure the Nation making the concessions; by unnecessarily parting with what ought to have been retained; and by exciting jealousy, ill-will, and a disposition to retaliate, in the parties from whom equal privileges are withheld. And it gives to ambitious, corrupted, or deluded citizens, (who devote themselves to the favorite nation,) facility to betray or sacrifice the interests of their own country, without odium, sometimes even with popularity; gilding, with the appearances of a virtuous sense of obligation, a commendable deference for public opinion, or a laudable zeal for public good, the base of foolish compliances of ambition, corruption, or infatuation.

As avenues to foreign influence in innumerable ways, such attachments are particularly alarming to the truly enlightened and independent Patriot. How many opportunities do they afford to tamper with domestic factions, to practise the arts of seduction, to mislead public opinion, to influence or awe the Public Councils! Such an attachment of a small or weak, towards a great and powerful nation, dooms the former to be the satellite of the latter.

Against the insidious wiles of foreign influence (I conjure you to believe me, fellow-citizens,) the jealousy of a free people ought to be *constantly* awake; since history and experience prove, that foreign influence is one of the most baneful foes of Republican Government. But that jealousy, to be useful, must be impartial; else it becomes the instrument of the very influence to be avoided, instead of a defence against it. Excessive partiality for one foreign nation, and excessive dislike of another, cause those whom they actuate to see danger only on one side, and serve to veil and even second the arts of influence on the other. Real patriots, who may resist the intrigues of the favorite, are liable to become suspected and odious; while its tools and dupes usurp the applause and confidence of the people, to surrender their interests.

The great rule of conduct for us, in regard to foreign nations, is, in extending our commercial relations, to have with them as little *political* connexion as possible. So far as we have already formed engagements, let them be fulfilled with perfect good faith. Here let us stop.

Europe has a set of primary interests, which to us have none, or a very remote relation. Hence she must be engaged in frequent controversies, the causes of which are essentially foreign to our concerns. Hence, therefore, it must be unwise in us to implicate ourselves, by artificial ties, in the ordinary vicissitudes of her politics, or the ordinary combinations and collisions of her friendships or enmities.

Our detached and distant situation invites and enables us to pursue a different course. If we remain one people, under an efficient government, the period is not far off, when we may defy material injury from external annoyance; when we may take such an attitude as will cause the neutrality, we may at any time resolve upon, to be scrupulously respected; when belligerent nations, under the impossibility of making acquisitions upon us, will not lightly hazard the giving us provocation; when we may choose peace or war, as our interest, guided by justice, shall counsel.

Why forego the advantages of so peculiar a situation? Why quit our own to stand upon foreign ground? Why, by interweaving our destiny with that of any part of Europe, entangle our peace and prosperity in the toils of European ambition, rivalship, interest, humor, or caprice?

It is our true policy to steer clear of permanent alliances with any portion of the foreign world; so far, I mean, as we are now at liberty to do it; for let me not be understood as capable of patronizing infidelity to existing engagements. I hold the maxim no less applicable to public than to private affairs, that honesty is always the best policy. I repeat it, therefore, let those engagements be observed in their genuine sense. But, in my opinion, it is unnecessary and would be unwise to extend them.

Taking care always to keep ourselves, by suitable establishments, on a respectable defensive posture, we may safely trust to temporary alliances for extraordinary emergencies.

Harmony, liberal intercourse with all nations, are recommended by policy, humanity, and interest. But even our commercial policy should hold an equal and impartial hand; neither seeking nor granting exclusive favors or preferences; consulting the natural course of things; diffusing and diversifying by gentle means the streams of commerce, but forcing nothing; establishing, with powers so disposed, in order to give trade a stable course, to define the rights of our merchants, and to enable the government to support them, conventional rules of intercourse, the best that present circumstances and mutual opinion will permit, but temporary, and liable to be from time to time abandoned or varied, as experience and circumstances shall dictate; constantly keeping in view, that it is folly in one nation to look for disinterested favors from another; that it must pay with a portion of its independence for whatever it may accept under that character; that, by such acceptance, it may place itself in the condition of having given equivalents for nominal favors, and yet of being reproached with ingratitude for not giving more. There can be no greater error than to expect or calculate upon real favors from nation to nation. It is an illusion, which experience must cure, which a just pride ought to discard.

In offering to you, my countrymen, these counsels of an old and affectionate friend, I dare not hope they will make the strong and lasting impression I could wish; that they will control the usual current of the passions, or prevent our nation from running the course, which has hitherto marked the destiny of nations. But, if I may even flatter myself, that they may be productive of some partial benefit, some occasional good; that they may now and then recur to moderate the fury of party spirit, to warn against the mischiefs of foreign intrigue, to guard against the impostures of pretended patriotism; this hope will be a full recompense for the solicitude for your welfare, by which they have been dictated.

How far in the discharge of my official duties, I have been guided by the principles which have been delineated, the public records and other evidences of my conduct must witness to you and to the world. To myself, the assurance of my own conscience is, that I have at least believed myself to be guided by them.

In relating to the still subsisting war in Europe, my Proclamation of the 22d of April, 1793, is the index to my Plan. Sanctioned by your approving voice, and by that of your Representatives in both Houses of Congress, the spirit of that measure has continually governed me, uninfluenced by any attempts to deter or divert me from it.

After deliberate examination, with the aid of the best lights I could obtain, I was well satisfied that our country, under all the circumstances of the case, had a right to take, and was bound in duty and interest to take, a neutral position. Having taken it, I determined, as far as should depend upon me, to maintain it, with moderation, perseverance, and firmness.

The considerations, which respect the right to hold this conduct, it is not necessary on this occasion to detail. I will only observe, that, according to my understanding of the matter, that right, so far from being denied by any of the Belligerent Powers, has been virtually admitted by all.

The duty of holding a neutral conduct may be inferred, without any thing more, from the obligation which justice and humanity impose on every nation, in cases in which it is free to act, to maintain inviolate the relations of peace and amity towards other nations.

The inducements of interest for observing that conduct will best be referred to your own reflections and experience. With me, a predominant motive has been to endeavour to gain time to our country to settle and mature its yet recent institutions, and to progress without interruption to that degree of strength and consistency, which is necessary to give it, humanly speaking, the command of its own fortunes.

Though, in reviewing the incidents of my administration, I am unconscious of intentional error, I am nevertheless too sensible of my defects not to think it probable that I may have committed many errors. Whatever they may be, I fervently beseech the Almighty to avert or mitigate the evils to which they may tend. I shall also carry with me the hope, that my Country will never cease to view them with indulgence; and that, after forty-five years of my life dedicated to its service with an upright zeal, the faults of incompetent abilities will be consigned to oblivion, as myself must soon be to the mansions of rest.

Relying on its kindness in this as in other things, and actuated by that fervent love towards it, which is so natural to a man, who views in it the native soil of himself and his progenitors for several generations; I anticipate with pleasing expectation that retreat, in which I promise myself to realize, without alloy, the sweet enjoyment of partaking, in the midst of my fellow-citizens, the benign influence of good laws under a free government, the ever favorite object of my heart, and the happy reward, as I trust, of our mutual cares, labors, and dangers.

GEORGE WASHINGTON.

United States, September 17th, 1796.

THE CONSTITUTION OF THE UNITED STATES

WE, the people of the United States, in order to form a more perfect union, establish justice, insure domestic tranquillity, provide for the common defense, promote the general welfare, and secure the blessings of liberty to ourselves and our posterity, do ordain and establish this Constitution for the United States of America.

ARTICLE I

SECTION I

All legislative powers herein granted shall be vested in a Congress of the United States, which shall consist of a Senate and House of Representatives.

SECTION II

The House of Representatives shall be composed of members chosen every second year by the people of the several States, and the electors in each State shall have the qualifications requisite for electors of the most numerous branch of the State legislature.

No person shall be a Representative who shall not have attained the age of twenty-five years, and been seven years a citizen of the United States, and who shall not, when elected, be an inhabitant of that State in which he shall be chosen.

Representatives and direct taxes shall be apportioned among the several States which may be included within this Union, according to their respective numbers, which shall be determined by adding to the whole number of free persons, including those bound to service for a term of years, and excluding Indians not taxed, three fifths of all other persons. The actual enumeration shall be made within three years after the first meeting of the Congress of the United States, and within every subsequent term of ten years, in such manner as they shall by law direct. The number of Representatives shall not exceed one for every thirty thousand, but each State shall have at least one Representative; and until such enumeration shall be made, the State of *New Hampshire* shall be entitled to choose three, *Massachusetts* eight, *Rhode Island and Providence Plantations* one, *Connecticut* five, *New York* six, *New Jersey* four, *Pennsylvania* eight, *Delaware* one, *Maryland* six, *Virginia* ten, *North Carolina* five, *South Carolina* five, and *Georgia* three.

When vacancies happen in the representation from any State, the executive authority thereof shall issue writs of election to fill such vacancies.

The House of Representatives shall choose their Speaker and other officers, and shall have the sole power of impeachment.

SECTION III

The Senate of the United States shall be composed of two Senators from each State, chosen by the legislature thereof, for six years; and each Senator shall have one vote.

Immediately after they shall be assembled in consequence of the first election, they shall be divided as equally as may be into three classes. The seats of the Senators of the first class shall be vacated at the expiration of the second year; of the second class, at the expiration of the fourth year, and of the third class, at the expiration of the sixth year, so that one third may be chosen every second year; and if vacancies happen by resignation or otherwise during the recess of the legislature of any State, the executive thereof may make temporary appointments until the next meeting of the legislature, which shall then fill such vacancies.

No person shall be a Senator who shall not have attained to the age of thirty years, and been nine years a citizen of the United States, and who shall not, when elected, be an inhabitant of that State for which he shall be chosen.

The Vice-President of the United States shall be President of the Senate, but shall have no vote, unless they be equally divided.

The Senate shall choose their other officers, and also a President *pro tempore* in the absence of the Vice-President, or when he shall exercise the office of President of the United States.

The Senate shall have the sole power to try all impeachments. When sitting for that purpose, they shall be on oath or affirmation. When the President of the United States is tried, the Chief Justice shall preside: and no person shall be convicted without the concurrence of two thirds of the members present.

Judgment in cases of impeachment shall not extend further than to removal from office, and disqualification to hold and enjoy any office of honor, trust, or profit under the United States; but the party convicted shall, nevertheless, be liable and subject to indictment, trial, judgment, and punishment, according to law.

103

SECTION IV

The times, places, and manner of holding elections for Senators and Representatives shall be prescribed in each State by the legislature thereof; but the Congress may at any time by law make or alter such regulations, except as to the places of choosing Senators.

The Congress shall assemble at least once in every year, and such meeting shall be on the first Monday in December, unless they shall by law appoint a different day.

SECTION V

Each house shall be the judge of the elections, returns, and qualifications of its own members, and a majority of each shall constitute a quorum to do business; but a smaller number may adjourn from day to day, and may be authorized to compel the attendance of absent members, in such manner, and under such penalties, as each house may provide.

Each house may determine the rules of its proceedings, punish its members for disorderly behavior, and with the concurrence of two thirds, expel a member.

Each house shall keep a journal of its proceedings, and from time to time publish the same, excepting such parts as may in their judgment require secrecy, and the yeas and nays of the members of either house on any question shall, at the desire of one fifth of those present, be entered on the journal.

Neither house, during the session of Congress, shall, without the consent of the other, adjourn for more than three days, nor to any other place than that in which the two houses shall be sitting.

SECTION VI

The Senators and Representatives shall receive a compensation for their services, to be ascertained by law and paid out of the Treasury of the United States. They shall, in all cases except treason, felony, and breach of the peace, be privileged from arrest during their attendance at the session of their respective houses, and in going to and returning from the same; and for any speech or debate in either house they shall not be questioned in any other place.

No Senator or Representative shall, during the time for which he was elected, be appointed to any civil office under the authority of the United States, which shall have been created, or the emoluments whereof shall have been increased during such time; and no person holding any office under the United States shall be a member of either house during his continuance in office.

SECTION VII

All bills for raising revenue shall originate in the House of Representatives; but the Senate may propose or concur with amendments as on other bills.

Every bill which shall have passed the House of Representatives and the Senate shall, before it become a law, be presented to the President of the United States; if he approve he shall sign it, but if not he shall return it, with his objections, to that house in which it shall have originated, who shall enter the objections at large on their journal and proceed to reconsider it. If after such reconsideration two thirds of that house shall agree to pass the bill, it shall be sent, together with the objections, to the other house, by which it shall likewise be reconsidered, and if approved by two thirds of that house it shall become a law. But in all such cases the votes of both houses shall be determined by yeas and nays, and the names of the persons voting for and against the bill shall be entered on the journal of each house respectively. If any bill shall not be returned by the President within ten days (Sundays excepted) after it shall have been presented to him, the same shall be a law, in like manner as if he had signed it, unless the Congress by their adjournment prevent its return, in which case it shall not be a law.

Every order, resolution, or vote to which the concurrence of the Senate and House of Representatives may be necessary (except on a question of adjournment) shall be presented to the President of the United States; and before the same shall take effect, shall be approved by him, or being disapproved by him, shall be repassed by two thirds of the Senate and House of Representatives, according to the rules and limitations prescribed in the case of a bill.

SECTION VIII

The Congress shall have power to lay and collect taxes, duties, imposts, and excises, to pay the debts and provide for the common defense and general welfare of the United States; but all duties, imposts, and excises shall be uniform throughout the United States;

To borrow money on the credit of the United States;

To regulate commerce with foreign nations and among the several States, and with the Indian tribes;

To establish an uniform rule of naturalization, and uniform laws on the subject of bankruptcies throughout the United States;

To coin money, regulate the value thereof, and of foreign coin, and fix the standard of weights and measures;

To provide for the punishment of counterfeiting the securities and current coin of the United States;

To establish post-offices and post-roads;

To promote the progress of science and useful arts by securing for limited times to authors and inventors the exclusive right to their respective writings and discoveries;

To constitute tribunals inferior to the Supreme Court;

To define and punish piracies and felonies committed on the high seas and offenses against the law of nations;

To declare war, grant letters of marque and reprisal, and make rules concerning captures on land and water;

To raise and support armies, but no appropriation of money to that use shall be for a longer term than two years;

To provide and maintain a navy;

To make rules for the government and regulation of the land and naval forces;

To provide for calling forth the militia to execute the laws of the Union, suppress insurrections, and repel invasions;

To provide for organizing, arming, and disciplining the militia, and for governing such part of them as may be employed in the service of the United States, reserving to the States respectively the appointment of the officers, and the authority of training the militia according to the discipline prescribed by Congress;

To exercise exclusive legislation in all cases whatsoever over such district (not exceeding ten miles square) as may, by cession of particular States and the acceptance of Congress, become the seat of the Government of the United States, and to exercise like authority over all places purchased by the consent of the legislature of the State in which the same shall be, for the erection of forts, magazines, arsenals, dockyards, and other needful buildings; and

APPENDIX

To make all laws which shall be necessary and proper for carrying into execution the foregoing powers, and all other powers vested by this Constitution in the Government of the United States, or in any department or officer thereof.

SECTION IX

The migration or importation of such persons as any of the States now existing shall think proper to admit shall not be prohibited by the Congress prior to the year one thousand eight hundred and eight, but a tax or duty may be imposed on such importation, not exceeding ten dollars for each person.

The privilege of the writ of habeas corpus shall not be suspended, unless when in cases of rebellion or invasion the public safety may require it.

No bill of attainder or ex post facto law shall be passed.

No capitation or other direct tax shall be laid, unless in proportion to the census or enumeration hereinbefore directed to be taken.

No tax or duty shall be laid on articles exported from any State.

No preference shall be given by any regulation of commerce or revenue to the ports of one State over those of another; nor shall vessels bound to or from one State be obliged to enter, clear, or pay duties in another.

No money shall be drawn from the Treasury but in consequence of appropriations made by law; and a regular statement and account of the receipts and expenditures of all public money shall be published from time to time.

No title of nobility shall be granted by the United States; and no person holding any office of profit or trust under them shall, without the consent of the Congress, accept of any present, emolument, office, or title, of any kind whatever, from any king, prince, or foreign State.

SECTION X

No State shall enter into any treaty, alliance, or confederation; grant letters of marque and reprisal; coin money; emit bills of credit; make anything but gold and silver coin a tender in payment of debts; pass any bill of attainder, ex post facto law, or law impairing the obligation of contracts, or grant any title of nobility.

No State shall, without the consent of Congress, lay any imposts or duties on imports or exports, except what may be absolutely necessary for executing its inspection laws; and the net
produce of all duties and imposts, laid by any State on imports
or exports, shall be for the use of the Treasury of the United
States; and all such laws shall be subject to the revision and
control of the Congress.

No State shall, without the consent of Congress, lay any duty
of tonnage, keep troops or ships of war in time of peace, enter
into any agreement or compact with another State or with a
foreign power, or engage in war, unless actually invaded or in
such imminent danger as will not admit of delay.

ARTICLE II

SECTION I

The executive power shall be vested in a President of the
United States of America. He shall hold his office during the
term of four years, and together with the Vice-President, chosen
for the same term, be elected as follows:

Each State shall appoint, in such manner as the legislature
thereof may direct, a number of electors, equal to the whole
number of Senators and Representatives to which the State may
be entitled in the Congress; but no Senator or Representative,
or person holding an office of trust or profit under the United
States, shall be appointed an elector.

[The electors shall meet in their respective States and vote
by ballot for two persons, of whom one at least shall not be an
inhabitant of the same State with themselves. And they shall
make a list of all the persons voted for, and of the number of
votes for each; which list they shall sign and certify, and transmit sealed to the seat of government of the United States, directed to the President of the Senate. The President of the
Senate shall, in the presence of the Senate and House of Representatives, open all the certificates, and the votes shall then
be counted. The person having the greatest number of votes
shall be the President, if such number be a majority of the whole
number of electors appointed; and if there be more than one
who have such majority, and have an equal number of votes,
then the House of Representatives shall immediately choose
by ballot one of them for President; and if no person have a

majority, then from the five highest on the list the said House shall in like manner choose the President. But in choosing the President the votes shall be taken by States, the representation from each State having one vote; a quorum for this purpose shall consist of a member or members from two thirds of the States, and a majority of all the States shall be necessary to a choice. In every case, after the choice of the President, the person having the greatest number of votes of the electors shall be the Vice-President. But if there should remain two or more who have equal votes, the Senate shall choose from them by ballot the Vice-President.][1]

The Congress may determine the time of choosing the electors and the day on which they shall give their votes, which day shall be the same throughout the United States.

No person except a natural-born citizen, or a citizen of the United States at the time of the adoption of this Constitution, shall be eligible to the office of President; neither shall any person be eligible to that office who shall not have attained to the age of thirty-five years, and been fourteen years a resident within the United States.

In case of the removal of the President from office, or of his death, resignation, or inability to discharge the powers and duties of the said office, the same shall devolve on the Vice-President, and the Congress may by law provide for the case of removal, death, resignation, or inability, both of the President and Vice-President, declaring what officer shall then act as President, and such officer shall act accordingly until the disability be removed or a President shall be elected.

The President shall, at stated times, receive for his services a compensation, which shall neither be increased nor diminished during the period for which he may have been elected, and he shall not receive within that period any other emolument from the United States or any of them.

Before he enter on the execution of his office he shall take the following oath or affirmation:

"I do solemnly swear (or affirm) that I will faithfully execute the office of President of the United States, and will to the best of my ability preserve, protect, and defend the Constitution of the United States."

---

[1] This clause of the Constitution has been amended. See twelfth article of the amendments.

SECTION II

The President shall be Commander-in-chief of the Army and Navy of the United States, and of the militia of the several States when called into the actual service of the United States; he may require the opinion, in writing, of the principal officer in each of the executive departments, upon any subject relating to the duties of their respective offices, and he shall have power to grant reprieves and pardons for offenses against the United States, except in cases of impeachment.

He shall have power, by and with the advice and consent of the Senate, to make treaties, provided two thirds of the Senators present concur; and he shall nominate, and, by and with the advice and consent of the Senate, shall appoint ambassadors, other public ministers and consuls, judges of the Supreme Court, and all other officers of the United States, whose appointments are not herein otherwise provided for, and which shall be established by law; but the Congress may by law vest the appointment of such inferior officers, as they think proper, in the President alone, in the courts of law, or in the heads of departments.

The President shall have power to fill up all vacancies that may happen during the recess of the Senate, by granting commissions which shall expire at the end of their next session.

SECTION III

He shall from time to time give to the Congress information of the state of the Union, and recommend to their consideration such measures as he shall judge necessary and expedient; he may, on extraordinary occasions, convene both houses, or either of them, and in case of disagreement between them with respect to the time of adjournment, he may adjourn them to such time as he shall think proper; he shall receive ambassadors and other public ministers; he shall take care that the laws be faithfully executed, and shall commission all the officers of the United States.

SECTION IV

The President, Vice-President, and all civil officers of the United States shall be removed from office on impeachment for and conviction of treason, bribery, or other high crimes and misdemeanors.

APPENDIX

ARTICLE III

SECTION I

The judicial power of the United States shall be vested in one Supreme Court, and in such inferior courts as the Congress may from time to time ordain and establish. The judges, both of the supreme and inferior courts, shall hold their offices during good behavior, and shall, at stated times, receive for their services a compensation which shall not be diminished during their continuance in office.

SECTION II

The judicial power shall extend to all cases, in law and equity, arising under this Constitution, the laws of the United States, and treaties made, or which shall be made, under their authority; to all cases affecting ambassadors, other public ministers, and consuls; to all cases of admiralty and maritime jurisdiction; to controversies to which the United States shall be a party; to controversies between two or more States; between a State and citizens of another State; between citizens of different States; between citizens of the same State claiming lands under grants of different States, and between a State, or the citizens thereof, and foreign States, citizens, or subjects.

In all cases affecting ambassadors, other public ministers and consuls, and those in which a State shall be a party, the Supreme Court shall have original jurisdiction. In all the other cases before mentioned the Supreme Court shall have appellate jurisdiction, both as to law and fact, with such exceptions and under such regulations as the Congress shall make.

The trial of all crimes, except in cases of impeachment, shall be by jury; and such trial shall be held in the State where the said crimes shall have been committed; but when not committed within any State, the trial shall be at such place or places as the Congress may by law have directed.

SECTION III

Treason against the United States shall consist only in levying war against them, or in adhering to their enemies, giving them aid and comfort. No person shall be convicted of treason unless on the testimony of two witnesses to the same overt act, or on confession in open court.

111

The Congress shall have power to declare the punishment of treason, but no attainder of treason shall work corruption of blood or forfeiture except during the life of the person attainted.

ARTICLE IV

SECTION I

Full faith and credit shall be given in each State to the public acts, records, and judicial proceedings of every other State. And the Congress may by general laws prescribe the manner in which such acts, records, and proceedings shall be proved, and the effect thereof.

SECTION II

The citizens of each State shall be entitled to all privileges and immunities of citizens in the several States.

A person charged in any State with treason, felony, or other crime, who shall flee from justice, and be found in another State, shall, on demand of the executive authority of the State from which he fled, be delivered up, to be removed to the State having jurisdiction of the crime.

No person held to service or labor in one State, under the laws thereof, escaping into another, shall, in consequence of any law or regulation therein, be discharged from such service or labor, but shall be delivered up on claim of the party to whom such service or labor may be due.

SECTION III

New States may be admitted by the Congress into this Union; but no new State shall be formed or erected within the jurisdiction of any other State; nor any State be formed by the junction of two or more States or parts of States, without the consent of the legislatures of the States concerned as well as of the Congress.

The Congress shall have power to dispose of and make all needful rules and regulations respecting the territory or other property belonging to the United States; and nothing in this Constitution shall be so construed as to prejudice any claims of the United States or of any particular State.

SECTION IV

The United States shall guarantee to every State in this Union a republican form of government, and shall protect each of them against invasion, and on application of the legislature, or of the executive (when the legislature cannot be convened), against domestic violence.

ARTICLE V

The Congress, whenever two thirds of both houses shall deem it necessary, shall propose amendments to this Constitution, or, on the Application of the Legislatures of two thirds of the several States, shall call a Convention for proposing Amendments, which, in either Case, shall be valid to all Intents and Purposes, as Part of this Constitution, when ratified by the Legislatures of three fourths of the several States, or by Conventions in three fourths thereof, as the one or the other Mode of Ratification may be proposed by the Congress; Provided [that no Amendment which may be made prior to the Year One thousand eight hundred and eight shall in any Manner affect the first and fourth Clauses in the Ninth Section of the first Article; and][2] that no State, without its Consent, shall be deprived of its equal Suffrage in the Senate.

ARTICLE VI

[§ 1.] All Debts contracted and Engagements entered into, before the Adoption of this Constitution, shall be as valid against the United States under this Constitution, as under the Confederation.[3]

[§ 2.] This Constitution, and the Laws of the United States which shall be made in Pursuance thereof; and all Treaties made, or which shall be made, under the Authority of the United States, shall be the supreme Law of the Land; and the Judges in every State shall be bound thereby, any Thing in the Constitution or Laws of any State to the Contrary notwithstanding.

[§ 3.] The Senators and Representatives before mentioned, and the Members of the several State Legislatures, and all executive and judicial Officers, both of the United States and of the several States, shall be bound by Oath or Affirmation, to support this Constitution; but no religious Test shall ever be required as a Qualification to any Office or public Trust under the United States.

---

[2] Temporary provision.
[3] Extended by Fourteenth Amendment, Section 4.

THE AMERICAN CANON

ARTICLE VII

The Ratification of the Conventions of nine States, shall be sufficient for the Establishment of this Constitution between the States so ratifying the Same.

AMENDMENTS[4]

[ARTICLE I][5]

Congress shall make no law respecting an establishment of religion, or prohibiting the free exercise thereof; or abridging the freedom of speech, or of the press; or the right of the people peaceably to assemble, and to petition the Government for a redress of grievances.

[ARTICLE II]

A well regulated Militia, being necessary to the security of a free State, the right of the people to keep and bear Arms, shall not be infringed.

[ARTICLE III]

No Soldier shall, in time of peace, be quartered in any house, without the consent of the Owner, nor in time of war, but in a manner to be prescribed by law.

[ARTICLE IV]

The right of the people to be secure in their persons, houses, papers, and effects, against unreasonable searches and seizures, shall not be violated, and no Warrants shall issue, but upon probable cause, supported by Oath or affirmation, and particularly describing the place to be searched, and the person or things to be seized.

[ARTICLE V]

No person shall be held to answer for a capital, or otherwise

[4] Amendments I to XX were ratified by legislatures; Amendment XXI was ratified by conventions as provided in the text of that particular "article."
[5] Amendments I to X were proposed by the Congress September 25, 1789, and on December 30, 1791, the President declared them ratified by eleven of the fourteen States. Apparently there was no action on the part of Connecticut, Georgia, or Massachusetts. In the original manuscripts the first twelve amendments have no numbers.

infamous crime, unless on a presentment or indictment of a Grand Jury, except in cases arising in the land or naval forces, or in the Militia, when in actual service in time of War or public danger; nor shall any person be subject for the same offence to be twice put in jeopardy of life or limb; nor shall be compelled in any criminal case to be a witness against himself, nor be deprived of life, liberty, or property, without due process of law; nor shall private property be taken for public use, without just compensation.

[ARTICLE VI]

In all criminal prosecutions the accused shall enjoy the right to a speedy and public trial, by an impartial jury of the State and district wherein the crime shall have been committed, which district shall have been previously ascertained by law, and to be informed of the nature and cause of the accusation; to be confronted with the witnesses against him; to have compulsory process for obtaining witnesses in his favor, and to have the Assistance of Counsel for his defence.

[ARTICLE VII]

In Suits at common law, where the value in controversy shall exceed twenty dollars, the right of trial by jury shall be preserved, and no fact tried by a jury shall be otherwise re-examined in any Court of the United States, than according to the rules of the common law.

[ARTICLE VIII]

Excessive bail shall not be required, nor excessive fines imposed, nor cruel and unusual punishments inflicted.

[ARTICLE IX]

The enumeration in the Constitution, of certain rights shall not be construed to deny or disparage others retained by the people.

[ARTICLE X]

The powers not delegated to the United States by the Constitution, nor prohibited by it to the States, are reserved to the States respectively or to the people.

[ARTICLE XI][6]

The Judicial power of the United States shall not be construed to extend to any suit in law or equity, commenced or prosecuted against one of the United States by Citizens of another State, or by Citizens or Subjects of any Foreign State.

[ARTICLE XII][7]

The Electors shall meet in their respective states, and vote by ballot for President and Vice-President, one of whom, at least, shall not be an inhabitant of the same state with themselves; they shall name in their ballots the person voted for as President, and in distinct ballots the person voted for as Vice-President, and they shall make distinct lists of all persons voted for as President and of all persons voted for as Vice-President, and of the number of votes for each, which lists they shall sign and certify, and transmit sealed to the seat of the government of the United States, directed to the President of the Senate;—The President of the Senate shall, in the presence of the Senate and House of Representatives, open all the certificates and the votes shall then be counted;—The person having the greatest number of votes for President, shall be the President, if such number be a majority of the whole number of Electors appointed; and if no person have such majority, then from the persons having the highest numbers not exceeding three on the list of those voted for as President, the House of Representatives shall choose immediately, by ballot, the President. But in choosing the President the votes shall be taken by States, the representation from each State having one vote; a quorum for this purpose shall consist of a member or members from two-thirds of the States, and a majority of all the States shall be necessary to a choice. And if the House of Representatives shall not choose a President whenever the right of choice shall devolve upon them, before the fourth day of March next following, then the Vice-President shall act as President, as in the case of the death or other constitutional disability of the President.—The person having the greatest number of votes as Vice-President shall

---

[6] The Eleventh Amendment was proposed by the Congress March 4, 1794, and on January 8, 1798, it was declared ratified by thirteen of the sixteen States. It was rejected by New Jersey and Pennsylvania.

[7] The Twelfth Amendment was proposed by the Congress December 8, 1803, and on September 25, 1804, its ratification by twelve of the seventeen States was proclaimed in Washington. Connecticut rejected it.

be the Vice-President, if such number be a majority of the whole number of Electors appointed, and if no person have a majority, then from the two highest numbers on the list, the Senate shall choose the Vice-President; a quorum for the purpose shall consist of two-thirds of the whole number of Senators, and a majority of the whole number shall be necessary to a choice. But no person constitutionally ineligible to the office of President shall be eligible to that of Vice-President of the United States.

[ARTICLE XIII][8]

SECTION 1. Neither slavery nor involuntary servitude, except as a punishment for crime whereof the party shall have been duly convicted, shall exist within the United States, or any place subject to their jurisdiction.

SECTION 2. Congress shall have power to enforce this article by appropriate legislation.

[ARTICLE XIV][9]

SECTION 1. All persons born or naturalized in the United States, and subject to the jurisdiction thereof, are citizens of the United States and of the State wherein they reside. No State shall make or enforce any law which shall abridge the privileges or immunities of citizens of the United States; nor shall any State deprive any person of life, liberty, or property, without due process of law; nor deny to any person within its jurisdiction the equal protection of the laws.

SECTION 2. Representatives shall be apportioned among the several States according to their respective numbers, counting the whole number of persons in each State, excluding Indians not taxed. But when the right to vote at any election for the choice of electors for President and Vice-President of the United States, Representatives in Congress, the Executive and Judicial officers

---

[8] The Thirteenth Amendment was proposed by resolution of the Congress, approved by the President on February 1, 1865, and on December 18, 1865, it was declared ratified by twenty-seven of the thirty-six States. Later it was ratified by six more States. Delaware and Mississippi rejected it.

[9] The Fourteenth Amendment was proposed by the Congress June 13, 1866, and by concurrent resolution of the Senate and the House of Representatives it was declared ratified by "three-fourths and more of the several States of the Union." A proclamation issued July 28, 1868, confirmed the ratification by thirty of the thirty-seven States. Later there were three more States that joined in the ratification. Delaware, Kentucky, and Maryland voted to reject.

of a State, or the members of the Legislature thereof, is denied to any of the male inhabitants of such State, being twenty-one years of age, and citizens of the United States, or in any way abridged, except for participation in rebellion, or other crime, the basis of representation therein shall be reduced in the proportion which the number of such male citizens shall bear to the whole number of male citizens twenty-one years of age in such State.

SECTION 3. No person shall be a Senator or Representative in Congress, or elector of President and Vice-President, or hold any office, civil or military, under the United States, or under any State, who, having previously taken an oath as a member of Congress, or as an officer of the United States, or as a member of any State legislature, or as an executive or judicial officer of any State, to support the Constitution of the United States, shall have engaged in insurrection or rebellion against the same, or given aid or comfort to the enemies thereof: But Congress may by a vote of two-thirds of each House, remove such disability.

SECTION 4. The validity of the public debt of the United States, authorized by law, including debts incurred for payment of pensions and bounties for services in suppressing insurrection or rebellion, shall not be questioned. But neither the United States nor any State shall assume or pay any debt or obligation incurred in aid of insurrection or rebellion against the United States, or any claim for the loss or emancipation of any slave; but all such debts, obligations and claims shall be held illegal and void.

SECTION 5. The Congress shall have power to enforce, by appropriate legislation, the provisions of this article.

[ARTICLE XV][10]

SECTION 1. The right of citizens of the United States to vote shall not be denied or abridged by the United States or by any State on account or race, color, or previous condition of servitude.

SECTION 2. The Congress shall have power to enforce this article by appropriate legislation.

[10] The Fifteenth Amendment was proposed by the Congress February 26, 1869. A proclamation dated March 30, 1870, announced the ratification by twenty-nine of the thirty-seven States. Later there were two more States to join in the ratification. California, Delaware, and Kentucky voted to reject.

APPENDIX

[ARTICLE XVI][11]

The Congress shall have power to lay and collect taxes on incomes, from whatever source derived, without apportionment among the several States, and without regard to any census or enumeration.

[ARTICLE XVII][12]

The Senate of the United States shall be composed of two Senators from each State, elected by the people thereof, for six years; and each Senator shall have one vote. The electors in each State shall have the qualifications requisite for electors of the most numerous branch of the State legislatures.

When vacancies happen in the representation of any State in the Senate, the executive authority of such State shall issue writs of election to fill such vacancies: *Provided*, That the legislature of any State may empower the executive thereof to make temporary appointments until the people fill the vacancies by election as the legislature may direct.

This amendment shall not be so construed as to affect the election or term of any Senator chosen before it becomes valid as part of the Constitution.

[ARTICLE XVIII][13]

SECTION 1. After one year from the ratification of this article the manufacture, sale, or transportation of intoxicating liquors within, the importation thereof into, or the exportation thereof from the United States and all territory subject to the jurisdiction thereof for beverage purposes is hereby prohibited.

[11] The Sixteenth Amendment was proposed by the Congress July 12, 1909, and its ratification by thirty-eight of the forty-eight States was announced on February 25, 1913. Later, four more States joined in ratification. Connecticut, Rhode Island, and Utah voted to reject.

[12] The Seventeenth Amendment was proposed by the Congress May 13, 1912, and its ratification by thirty-six of the forty-eight States was proclaimed on May 31, 1913. Later, one more State added its ratification. Utah rejected it.

[13] The Eighteenth Amendment was proposed by the Congress December 18, 1917, and its ratification by thirty-six of the forty-eight States was proclaimed January 29, 1919. Later, ten more States added their votes of ratification. Apparently Connecticut and Rhode Island took no action. Ratification by the thirty-sixth State was completed on January 16, 1919, and the Amendment therefore became effective January 16, 1920. Repeal of the Eighteenth Amendment was proclaimed December 5, 1933.

SECTION 2. The Congress and the several States shall have concurrent power to enforce this article by appropriate legislation.

SECTION 3. This article shall be inoperative unless it shall have been ratified as an amendment to the Constitution by the legislatures of the several States, as provided in the Constitution, within seven years from the date of the submission hereof to the States by the Congress.

[ARTICLE XIX][14]

The right of citizens of the United States to vote shall not be denied or abridged by the United States or by any State on account of sex.

Congress shall have the power to enforce this article by appropriate legislation.

[ARTICLE XX][15]

SECTION 1. The terms of the President and Vice-President shall end at noon on the twentieth day of January, and the terms of Senators and Representatives at noon on the third day of January, of the years in which such terms would have ended if this article had not been ratified; and the terms of their successors shall then begin.

SECTION 2. The Congress shall assemble at least once in every year, and such meeting shall begin at noon on the third day of January, unless they shall by law appoint a different day.

SECTION 3. If, at the time fixed for the beginning of the term of the President, the President elect shall have died, the Vice-President elect shall become President. If a President shall not have been chosen before the time fixed for the beginning of his term, or if the President elect shall have failed to qualify, then the Vice-President elect shall act as President until a President shall have qualified; and the Congress may by law provide for the case

[14] The Nineteenth Amendment was proposed by the Congress June 4, 1919, and its ratification by thirty-six of the forty-eight States was proclaimed August 26, 1920. Later, two more States added their ratifications. Alabama, Maryland, and Virginia voted to reject.

[15] The Twentieth Amendment was proposed by the Congress March 2, 1932, and its ratification by thirty-nine of the forty-eight States was proclaimed February 6, 1933. The other nine States added their ratifications before October 15, 1933, the day that Sections 1 and 2 became effective. The other sections of the Amendment went into effect on January 23, 1933, when ratification was completed by the thirty-sixth State.

wherein neither a President elect nor a Vice-President elect shall have qualified, declaring who shall then act as President, or the manner in which one who is to act shall be selected, and such person shall act accordingly until a President or Vice-President shall have qualified.

SECTION 4. The Congress may by law provide for the case of the death of any of the persons from whom the House of Representatives may choose a President whenever the right of choice shall have devolved upon them, and for the case of the death of any of the persons from whom the Senate may choose a Vice-President whenever the right of choice shall have devolved upon them.

SECTION 5. Sections 1 and 2 shall take effect on the fifteenth day of October following the ratification of this article.

SECTION 6. This article shall be inoperative unless it shall have been ratified as an amendment to the Constitution by the legislatures of three-fourths of the several States within seven years from the date of its submission.

[ARTICLE XXI][16]

SECTION 1. The eighteenth article of amendment to the Constitution of the United States is hereby repealed.

SECTION 2. The transportation or importation into any State, Territory, or possession of the United States for delivery or use therein of intoxicating liquors, in violation of the laws thereof, is hereby prohibited.

SECTION 3. This article shall be inoperative unless it shall have been ratified as an amendment to the Constitution by conventions in the several States, as provided in the Constitution, within seven years from the date of the submission hereof to the States by the Congress.

[16] The Twenty-first Amendment was proposed by the Congress February 20, 1933, and its ratification by conventions in thirty-six of the forty-eight States was proclaimed December 5, 1933. Later, one other State joined in the ratification. The convention in South Carolina voted to reject, and North Carolina voted against holding a convention.

THE DECLARATION OF INDEPENDENCE

In Congress, July 4, 1776

THE UNANIMOUS DECLARATION OF THE THIRTEEN UNITED STATES OF AMERICA

WHEN in the Course of human events, it becomes necessary for one people to dissolve the political bands which have connected them with another, and to assume among the Powers of the earth, the separate and equal station to which the Laws of Nature and of Nature's God entitle them, a decent respect to the opinions of mankind requires that they should declare the causes which impel them to the separation.

We hold these truths to be self-evident, that all men are created equal, that they are endowed by their Creator with certain unalienable Rights, that among these are Life, Liberty and the pursuit of Happiness. That to secure these rights, Governments are instituted among Men, deriving their just powers from the consent of the governed, That whenever any Form of Government becomes destructive of these ends, it is the Right of the People to alter or to abolish it, and to institute new Government, laying its foundation on such principles and organizing its powers in such form, as to them shall seem most likely to effect their Safety and Happiness. Prudence, indeed, will dictate that Governments long established should not be changed for light and transient causes; and accordingly all experience hath shown, that mankind are more disposed to suffer, while evils are sufferable, than to right themselves by abolishing the forms to which they are accustomed. But when a long train of abuses and usurpations, pursuing invariably the same Object evinces a design to reduce them under absolute Despotism, it is their right, it is their duty, to throw off such Government, and to provide new Guards for their future security.— Such has been the patient sufferance of these Colonies; and such is now the necessity which constrains them to alter their former Systems of Government. The history of the present King of Great Britain is a history of repeated injuries and usurpations, all having in direct object the establishment of an absolute Tyranny over these States. To prove this, let Facts be submitted to a candid world.

APPENDIX

He has refused his Assent to Laws, the most wholesome and necessary for the public good.

He has forbidden his Governors to pass Laws of immediate and pressing importance, unless suspended in their operation till his Assent should be obtained; and when so suspended, he has utterly neglected to attend to them.

He has refused to pass other Laws for the accommodation of large districts of people, unless those people would relinquish the right of Representation in the Legislature, a right inestimable to them and formidable to tyrants only.

He has called together legislative bodies at places unusual, uncomfortable, and distant from the depository of their Public Records, for the sole purpose of fatiguing them into compliance with his measures.

He has dissolved Representative Houses repeatedly, for opposing with manly firmness his invasions on the rights of the people.

He has refused for a long time, after such dissolutions, to cause others to be elected; whereby the Legislative Powers, incapable of Annihilation, have returned to the People at large for their exercise; the State remaining in the mean time exposed to all the dangers of invasion from without, and convulsions within.

He has endeavoured to prevent the population of these States; for that purpose obstructing the Laws for Naturalization of Foreigners; refusing to pass others to encourage their migration hither, and raising the conditions of new Appropriations of Lands.

He has obstructed the Administration of Justice, by refusing his Assent to Laws for establishing Judiciary Powers.

He has made Judges dependent on his Will alone, for the tenure of their offices, and the amount and payment of their salaries.

He has erected a multitude of New Offices, and sent hither swarms of Officers to harass our People, and eat out their substance.

He has kept among us, in times of peace, Standing Armies without the Consent of our legislature.

He has affected to render the Military independent of and superior to the Civil Power.

He has combined with others to subject us to a jurisdiction foreign to our constitution, and unacknowledged by our laws; giving his Assent to their Acts of pretended Legislation:

For quartering large bodies of armed troops among us:

For protecting them, by a mock Trial, from Punishment for any Murders which they should commit on the Inhabitants of these States:

123

For cutting off our Trade with all parts of the world:

For imposing taxes on us without our Consent:

For depriving us in many cases, of the benefits of Trial by Jury:

For transporting us beyond Seas to be tried for pretended offences:

For abolishing the free System of English Laws in a neighbouring Province, establishing therein an Arbitrary government, and enlarging its Boundaries so as to render it at once an example and fit instrument for introducing the same absolute rule into these Colonies:

For taking away our Charters, abolishing our most valuable Laws, and altering fundamentally the Forms of our Governments:

For suspending our own Legislatures, and declaring themselves invested with Power to legislate for us in all cases whatsoever.

He has abdicated Government here, by declaring us out of his Protection and waging War against us.

He has plundered our seas, ravaged our Coasts, burnt our towns, and destroyed the lives of our people.

He is at this time transporting large armies of foreign mercenaries to compleat the works of death, desolation and tyranny, already begun with circumstances of Cruelty & perfidy scarcely paralleled in the most barbarous ages, and totally unworthy the Head of a civilized nation.

He has constrained our fellow Citizens taken Captive on the high Seas to bear Arms against their Country, to become the executioners of their friends and Brethren, or to fall themselves by their Hands.

He has excited domestic insurrections amongst us, and has endeavoured to bring on the inhabitants of our frontiers, the merciless Indian Savages, whose known rule of warfare is an undistinguished destruction of all ages, sexes and conditions.

In every stage of these Oppressions We have Petitioned for Redress in the most humble terms: Our repeated Petitions have been answered only by repeated injury. A Prince, whose character is thus marked by every act which may define a Tyrant, is unfit to be the ruler of a free People.

Nor have We been wanting in attention to our British brethren. We have warned them from time to time of attempts by their legislature to extend an unwarrantable jurisdiction over us. We have reminded them of the circumstances of our emigration and settlement here. We have appealed to their native justice and magnanimity, and we have conjured them by the ties of our common kindred to disavow these usurpations, which, would inevitably interrupt our connections and correspondence. They too have been deaf to the voice of justice and of consanguinity. We must, therefore, acquiesce in the necessity, which denounces our Separation, and hold them, as we hold the rest of mankind, Enemies in War, in Peace Friends.

We, therefore, the Representatives of the united States of America, in General Congress, Assembled, appealing to the Supreme Judge of the world for the rectitude of our intentions, do, in the Name, and by Authority of the good People of these Colonies, solemnly publish and declare, That these United Colonies are, and of Right ought to be Free and Independent States; that they are Absolved from all Allegiance to the British Crown, and that all political connection between them and the State of Great Britain, is and ought to be totally dissolved; and that as Free and Independent States, they have full Power to levy War, conclude Peace, contract Alliances, establish Commerce, and to do all other Acts and Things which Independent States may of right do. And for the support of this Declaration, with a firm reliance on the Protection of Divine Providence, we mutually pledge to each other our Lives, our Fortunes and our sacred Honor.

THE MAYFLOWER COMPACT

In yᵉ name of God, Amen. We whose names are underwriten, the loyall subjects of our dread soveraigne Lord, King James, by yᵉ grace of God, of Great Britaine, Franc, & Ireland king, defender of yᵉ faith, &c., haveing undertaken, for yᵉ glorie of God, and advancemente of yᵉ Christian faith, and honour of our king & countrie, a voyage to plant yᵉ first colonie in yᵉ Northerne parts of Virginia, doe by these presents solemnly & mutualy in yᵉ presence of God, and one of another, covenant & combine our selves togeather into a civill body politick, for our better ordering & preservation & furtherance of yᵉ ends aforesaid; and by vertue hearof to enacte, constitute, and frame such just & equall lawes, ordinances, acts, constitutions, & offices, from time to time, as shall be thought most meete & convenient for yᵉ generall good of yᵉ Colonie, unto which we promise all due submission and obedience. In witnes wherof we have hereunder subscribed our names at Cap-Codd yᵉ 11. of November, in yᵉ year of yᵉ raigne of our soveraigne lord, King James, of England, France, & Ireland yᵉ eighteenth, and of Scotland yᵉ fiftie fourth. Anᵒ: Dom. 1620.